BEST OF THE WHO

Cover photos by JEFFREY MAYER

ISBN 0-634-02228-8

HAL•LEONARD®
CORPORATION
7777 W. BLUEMOUND RD. P.O. BOX 13819 MILWAUKEE, WI 53213

Visit Hal Leonard Online at
www.halleonard.com

P9-DCZ-602

BEST
THE W

Photo by HARRY GOODWIN

ATHENA

Words and Music by
PETER TOWNSHEND

Bright Rock

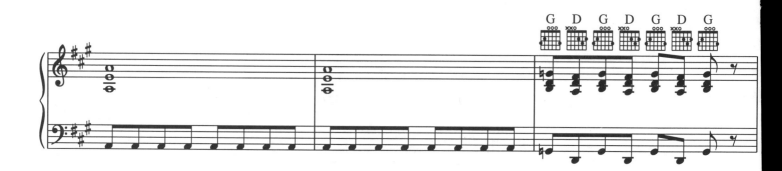

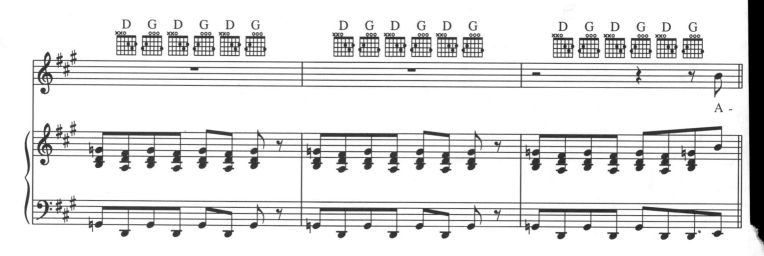

the - na, _____ I ____ had no i - dea ___ how much I'd
the - na, _____ all ___ I ev - er want __ to do is

need her. ___
please her. ___
In peace - ful times I hold her close ___ and I
My life has been so settled and she's the

feed her.
rea - son.
My heart starts pal - pi - ta - tin' when I think my
Just one word from her and my trou - bles are

guess was wrong, ___
long gone, _____
but I think I get a - long. _____
She's just a

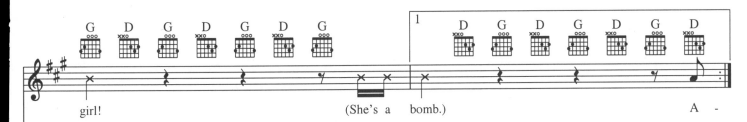

girl!
(She's a bomb.)
A -

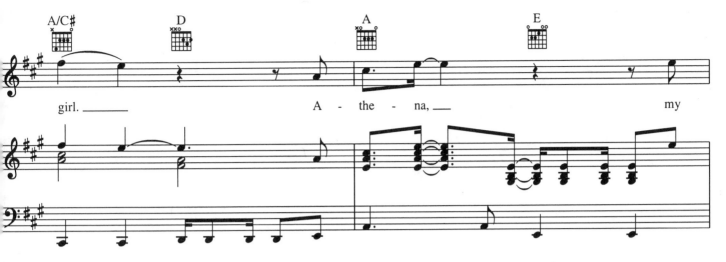

girl. _____ A - the - na, ___ my

heart felt like a shat-tered glass _ in an ac-id bath, _ felt like

one of those flat-tened ants _ you'd find on a cra-zy path. _ I'd-'ve

topped my-self to give her time, _ she did-n't need to ask. ___ Was I a

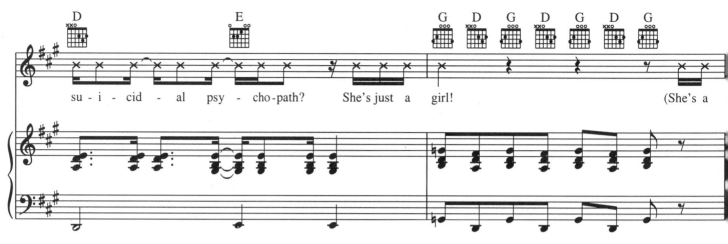

su-i-cid-al psy-cho-path? She's just a girl! (She's a

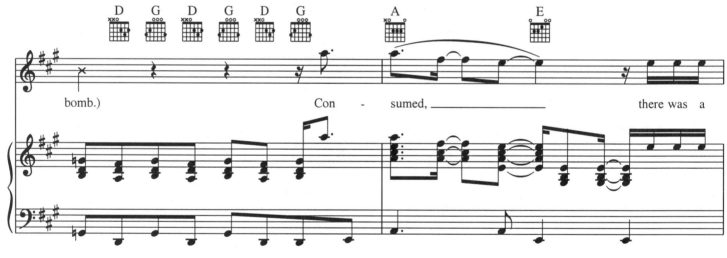

bomb.) She's just a girl! (She's a

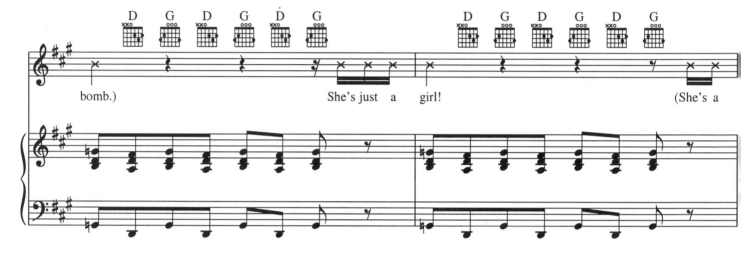

bomb.) Con-sumed, _____ there was a

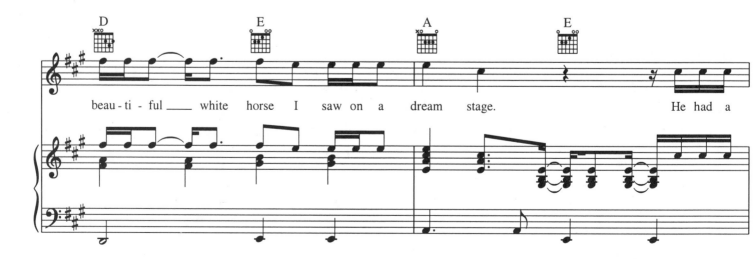

beau-ti-ful ____ white horse I saw on a dream stage. He had a

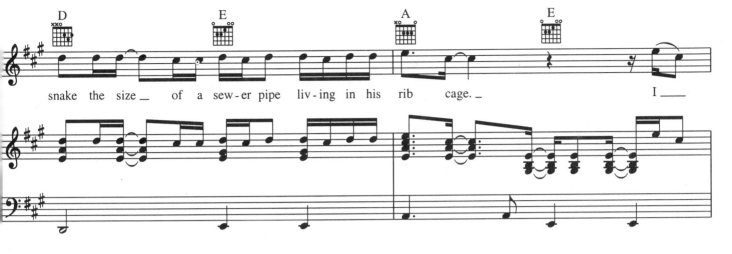

snake the size __ of a sew - er pipe liv - ing in his rib cage. __ I __

felt like a pick - led priest __ who was be - ing flam - beed. __ You got me

req - ui - si - tioned blonde - ie! She's just a girl! (She's a

D.S. al Coda

bomb.) (She's a bomb.)

Spoken: I'm happy! *Spoken: I'm ecstatic!*

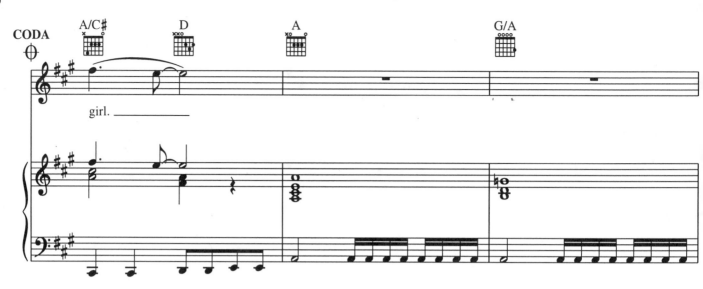

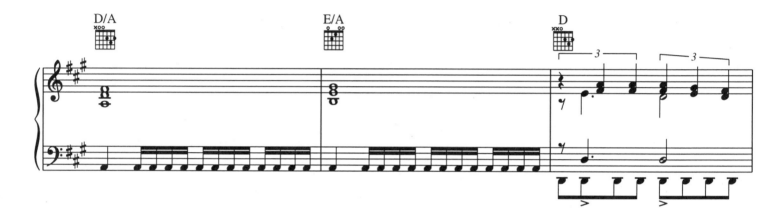

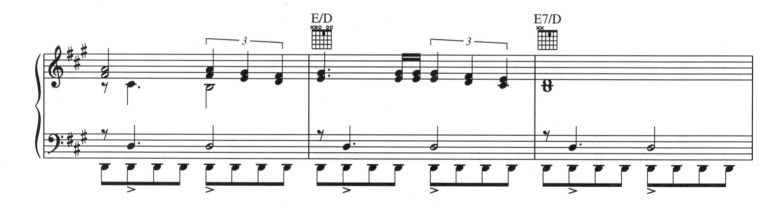

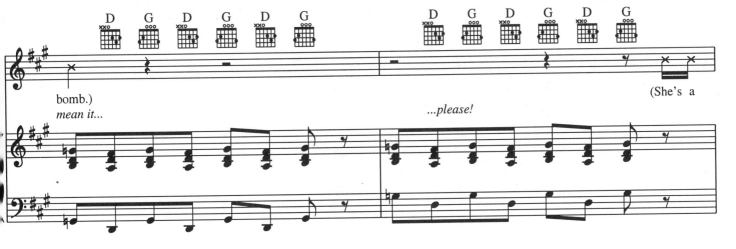

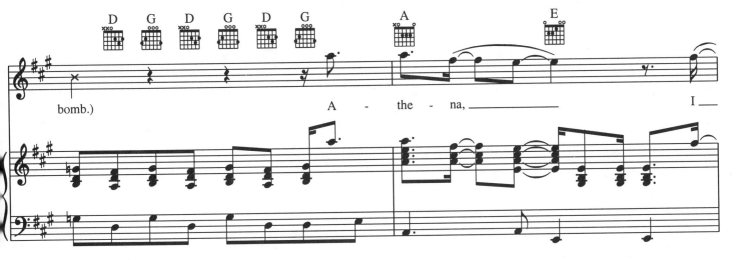

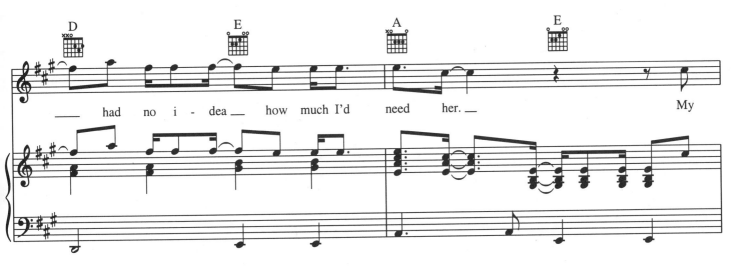

Just one word from her __ and my troub-les are long gone, __ but I

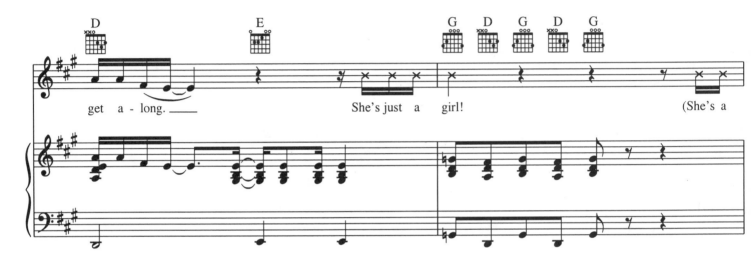

get a - long. __ She's just a girl! (She's a

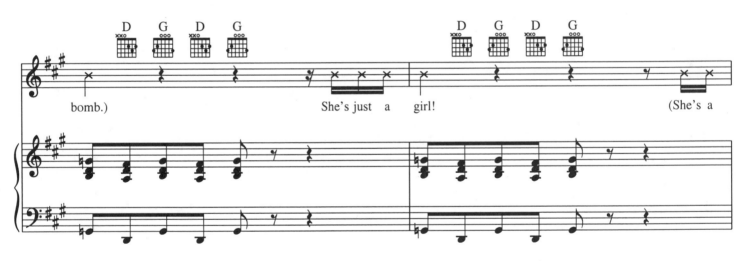

bomb.) She's just a girl! (She's a

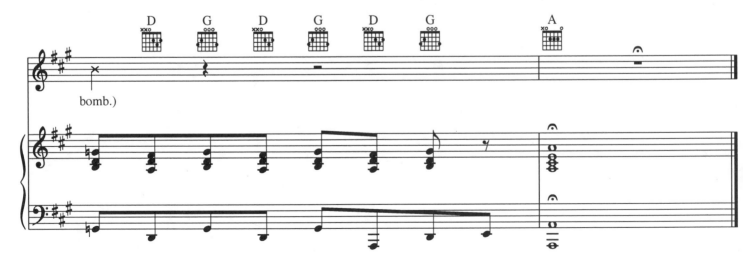

bomb.)

DOGS

Words and Music by
PETER TOWNSHEND

Bright Rock

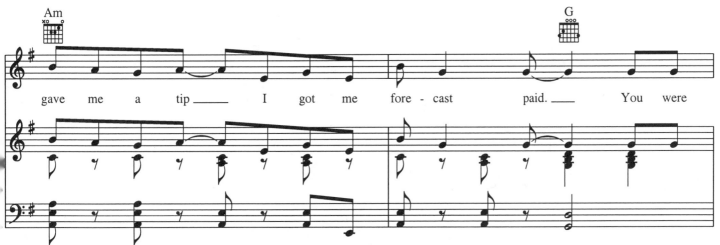

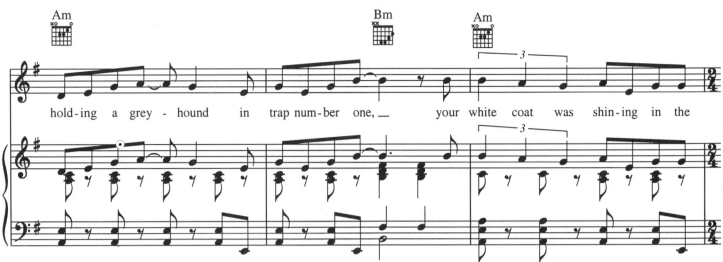

hold-ing a grey-hound in trap num-ber one, __ your white coat was shin-ing in the

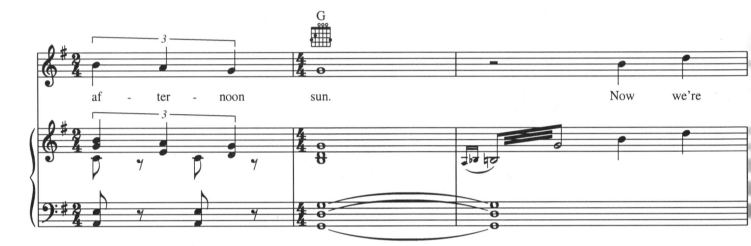

af - ter - noon sun. Now we're

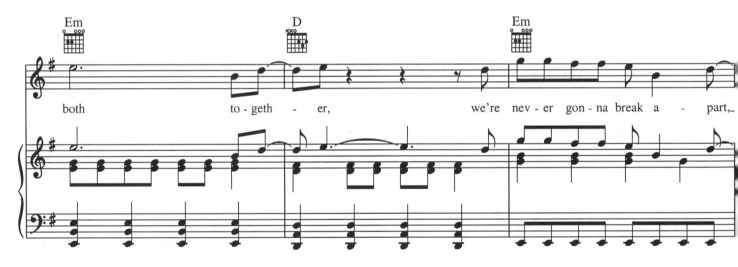

both to-geth - er, we're nev-er gon-na break a - part, __

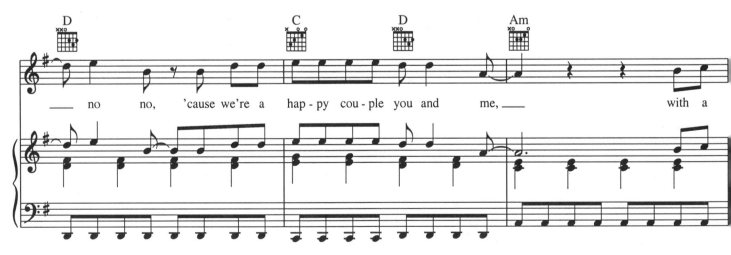

__ no no, 'cause we're a hap-py cou-ple you and me, __ with a

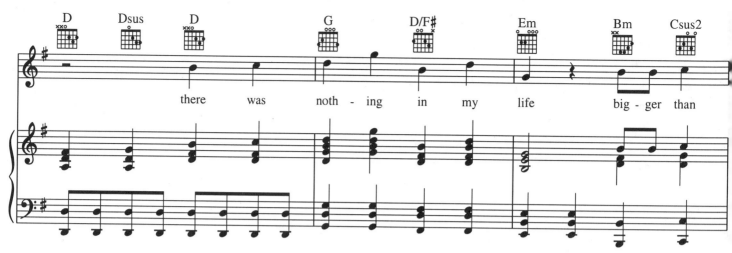

there was noth-ing in my life big-ger than

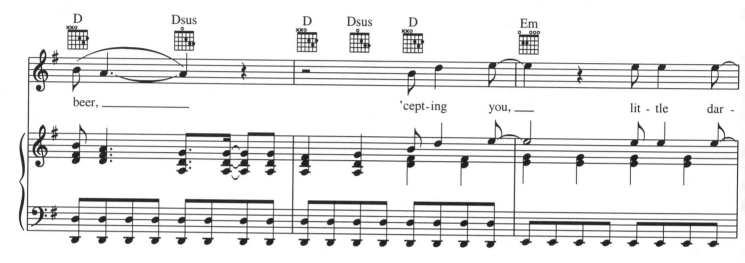

beer, _____ 'cept-ing you, ___ lit-tle dar-

-ling, 'cept-ing you, ___ lit-tle dar-ling, we're _ a hap-

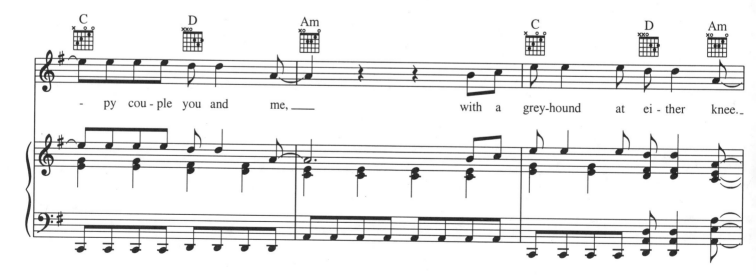

-py cou-ple you and me, ___ with a grey-hound at ei-ther knee. _

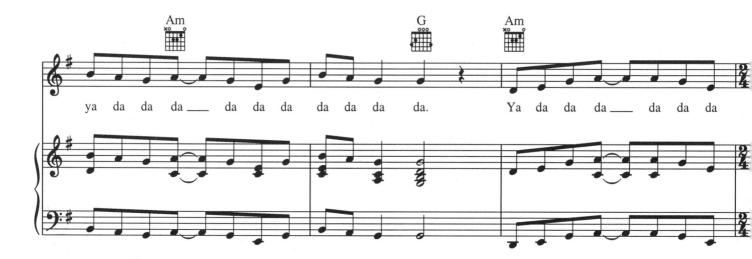

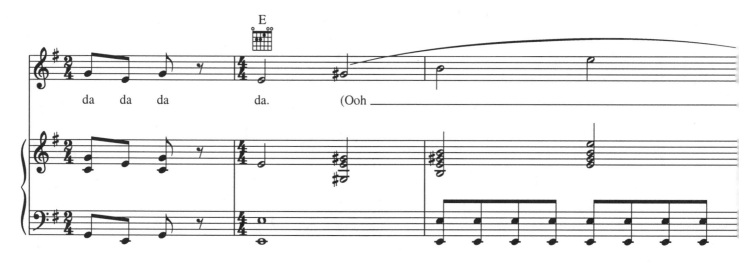

Spoken: Girl, where's me wage packet? Oh, ... ,
Ah I'll put twenty-five knicker please on Gallop Printer.
Oh, hope the wife don't find out.
Yes, it's sure to win, isn't it?
Yes, I know, it's a good dog. I saw it run at White City
just last week, -- broke the record. Gallop Printer,
nice dog, yes, lovely form, lovely buttocks...

BABA O'RILEY

Words and Music by
PETER TOWNSHEND

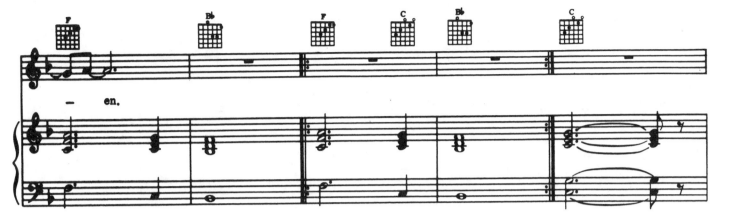

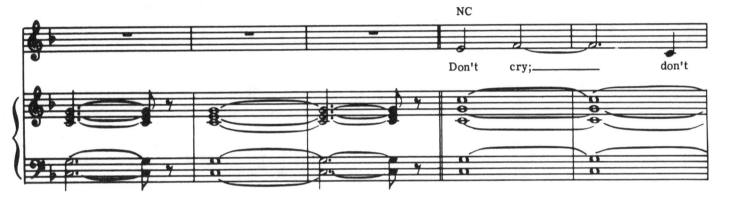

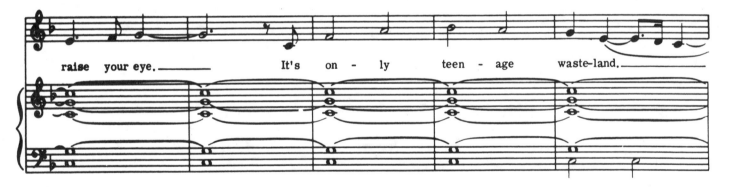

Put out the fire___ and don't look past___ my shoul - der.___

The ex - o - dus is here;___ The hap-py ones are near.___

Let's get to-geth - er be - fore we get___ much old - er.___

CHORUS

Teen - age

waste-land; It's on-ly teen - age waste-land. Teen-age waste-land;

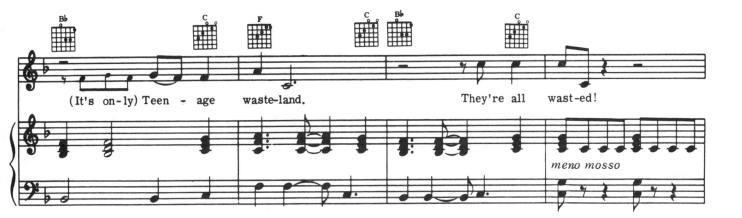

(It's on-ly) Teen - age waste-land. They're all wast-ed!

meno mosso

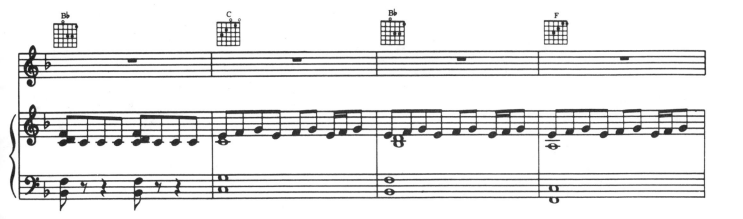

accel.

BARGAIN

Words and Music by
PETER TOWNSHEND

Bar-gain;____ The best I ev - er had. The

best I ev - er had._____ I'd

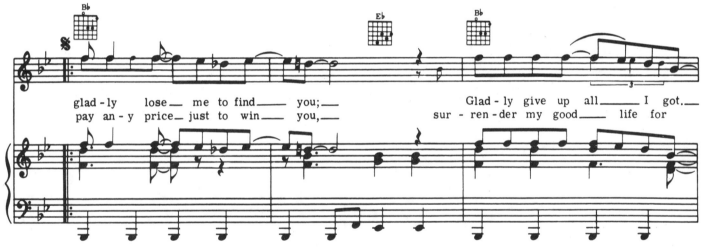

glad - ly lose__ me to find____ you;__ Glad - ly give up all____ I got.__
pay an - y price__ just to win__ you,__ sur - ren - der my good____ life for

____ To catch you,____ I'm gon-na run__ and nev-er stop.____
bad. To find you,____ I'm gon-na drown__ an un-sung man.____

I'd | I'd call that a Bar - gain; _____ The best I ev - er

had. | The best I ev - er had. _____

I sit look-in' 'round; _____ I look at my face

__ in the mir - ror; | I know I'm worth noth-ing _____ with-out _____ you.

BEHIND BLUE EYES

Words and Music by
PETER TOWNSHEND

fa - ted / pain and woe to tell - ing on - ly lies. / can show____ through. But my

dreams,_____ they aren't as emp-ty as my con - science

seems____ to be.____ I have ho - urs_____ on - ly lone-

- ly,____ My love is ven - geance____ that's nev - er

When my fist clen - ches, crack it op - en

be-fore I use__ it and lose__ my cool.__ When I smile,__ tell me some bad__

news be-fore I laugh and act like a fool.__ If I swal-

DON'T LET GO THE COAT

Words and Music b
PETER TOWNSHEN

Moderately

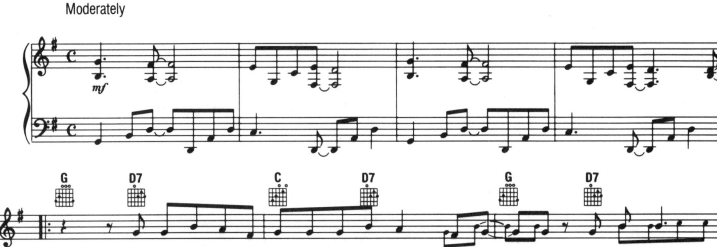

I can't be held re-spon-si-ble for blown be-hav-ior I lost all
It's eas-y to be sad when you lack a part-ner, But how would I re-

con-tact with my on-ly sav-ior No one locked me out be-cause I failed to phone
act to a bro-ken heart now. It ain't real-ly true rock and roll un-less

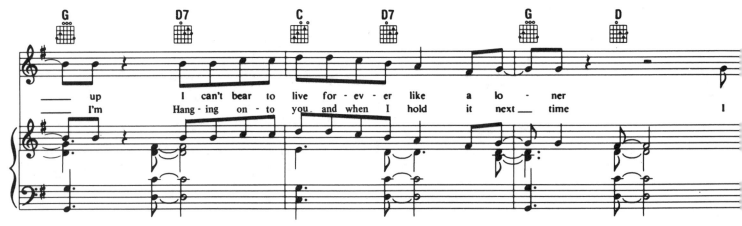

____ up I can't bear to live for-ev-er like a lo-ner
____ I'm Hang-ing on-to you and when I hold it next ____ time I

Don't let go ___ the coat. ___   Don't let go ___ the coat. ___
won't let go ___ the coat. ___   Don't let go ___ the coat. ___   Don't

Don't let go ___ the coat. ___   Don't let go ___ the coat. Don't let go ___ the coat.
let go ___ the coat.

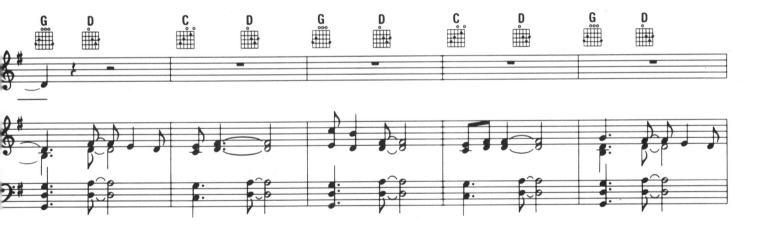

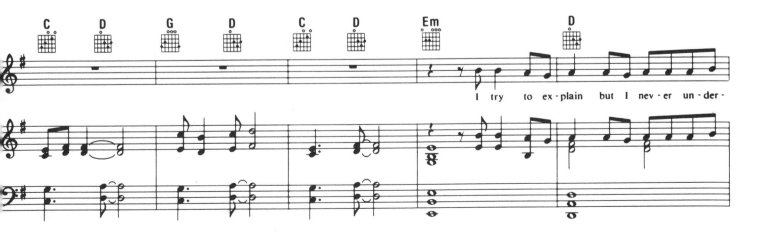

I try to ex-plain but I nev-er un-der-

stand it. I need your bod-y, but I can't just de-mand it.

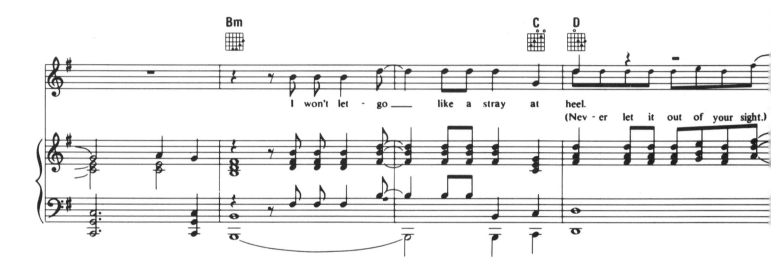

I won't let-go ___ like a stray at heel.
(Nev-er let it out of your sight.)

Ev-'ry lone-ly wife knows the way I feel.
(Don't let go ___ to-night

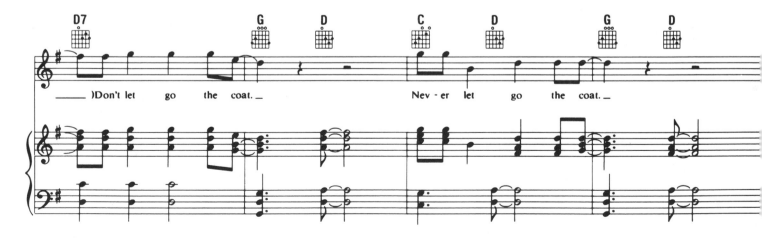

___)Don't let go the coat. ___ Nev-er let go the coat. ___

EMINENCE FRONT

Words and Music by
PETER TOWNSHEND

Moderate Rock

Fm7

Db(add9)

Play 3 times

Fm7

Db(add9)

The

sun   shines, _____ and peo-ple for-get. __
drinks   flow, _____ peo-ple for-get. __

It's an em - i - nence front.   It's an em - i - nence front. It's a put - on. _____

An em - i - nence front,   em - i - nence front,   put - on. _____

_____ Em - i - nence   front.

To Coda ⊕

It's an em - i - nence front. It's an em - i - nence front. It's a put - on. ___

It's a put - on. It's a put - on. It's a put - on.

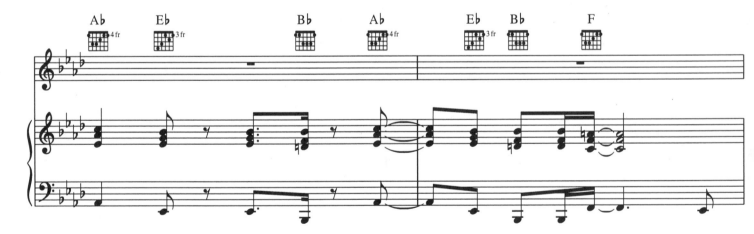

Come and join the par - ty, dress to

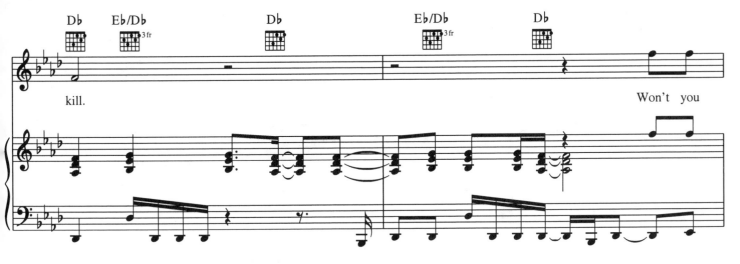

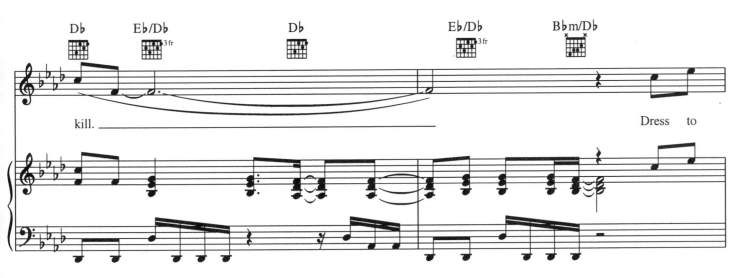

D.S. al Coda

The

CODA   Db(add9)

It's a put-on.   It's a put-on.   It's a put-on. _____

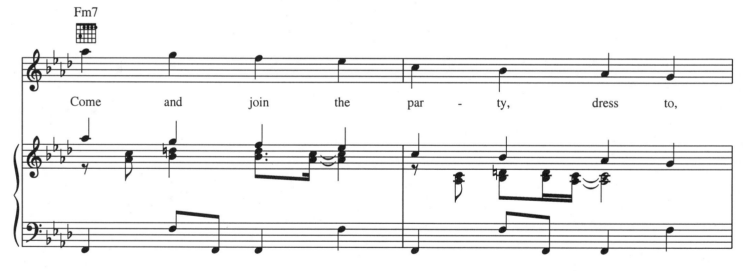

Fm7

Come   and   join   the   par - ty,   dress   to,

Db

come   and   join   the   par - ty,   dress   to, ____

come and join the par - ty, dress to,

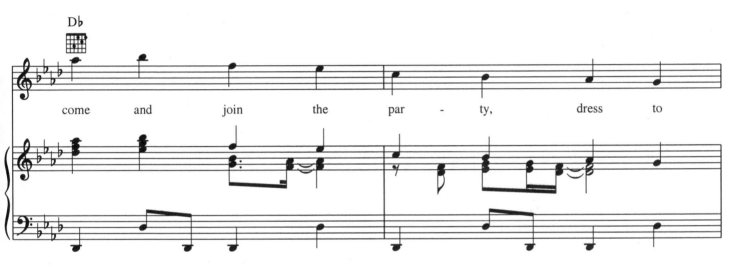

come and join the par - ty, dress to

kill.

Dress your-self __ to kill.

5:15

Words and Music by
PETER TOWNSHEND

Moderately fast

Why should I care?_____ Why_____ should I care?_____

Driving

_____ of fif - teen, sex - ual - ly know - ing, The ush - ers are sniff - ing, eau-

Girls

GOING MOBILE

Words and Music by
PETER TOWNSHEND

I'm go-in' home _____ and when I want to go home _____ I'm Go - in' Mo - bile.

Well, I'm gon - na find a home on wheels, ____ see how it feels, Go-in' Mo-bile.

Keep ___ me mov - in'. ____

I can pull up by the kerb, I can make it on the road, Go - in' Mo-bile.

I can stop in an - y street in-vit - in' peo-ple that we meet, Go-in' Mo - bile.___

Keep___ me mov - in'.___

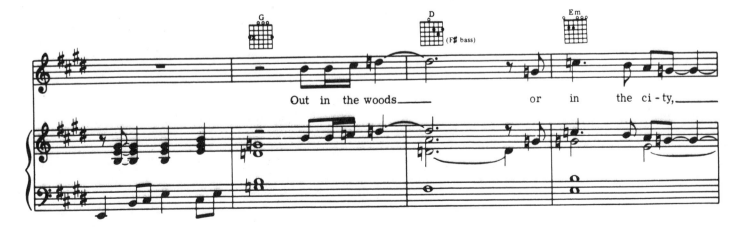

Out in the woods___ or in the ci - ty,___

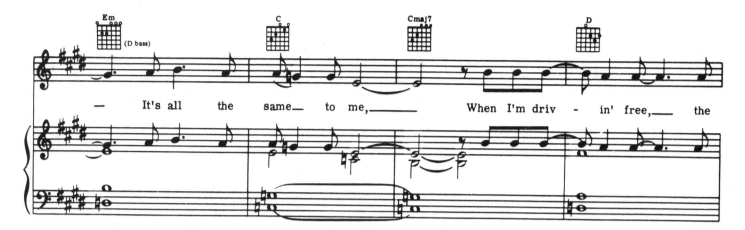

It's all the same— to me,—— When I'm driv - in' free,— the

world's my home,— When I'm mo - bile.

Play the tape ma-chine, make the toast and tea— when I'm mo-

— bile.— Well I can lay in bed—with on-ly high-way a-head,—when I'm mo-

bile. Keep __ me mov - in'. __

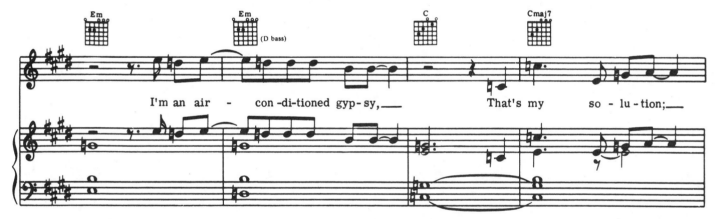

I don't care __ a-bout pol-lu -tion, __

I'm an air - con-di-tioned gyp-sy, __ That's my so - lu -tion; __

Watch the po - lice and the tax man miss __ me; I'm mo - bile! __

I CAN SEE FOR MILES

Words and Music by
PETER TOWNSHEND

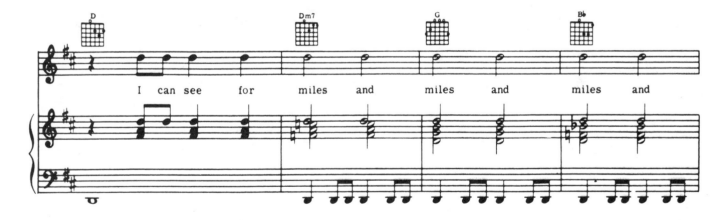

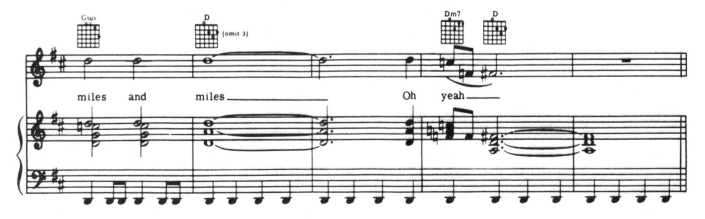

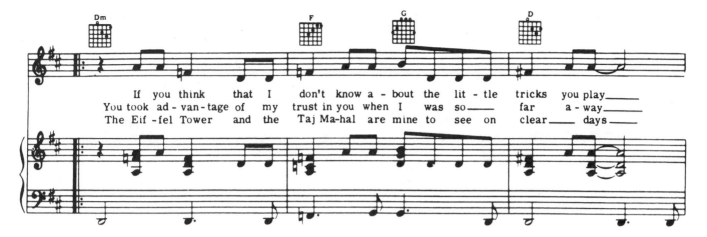

If you think that I don't know a-bout the lit-tle tricks you play___
You took ad-van-tage of my trust in you when I was so___ far a-way___
The Eif-fel Tower and the Taj Ma-hal are mine to see on clear___ days___

And nev-er see you when de - lib'-rate-ly you put things
I saw you hold-ing lots of oth - er guys and now you got the
You thought that I would need a crys-tal ball to see right

in my way___
nerve to say___
through the haze___

Well here's a poke at you.___ You're gon - na
That you still want me.___ Well___
Well here's a poke at you.___ You're gon - na

choke on it too.___ You're gon-na lose that smile___ Be - cause all the while___
that's as may be___ But you got-ta stand trial___ Be - cause all the while___
choke on it too.___ You're gon-na lose that smile___ Be - cause all the while___

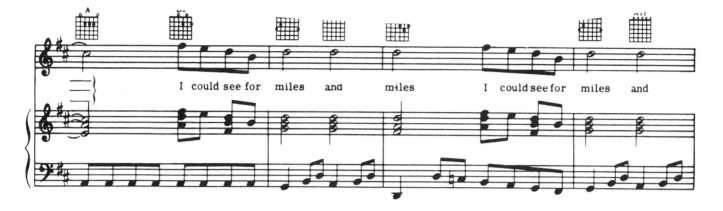

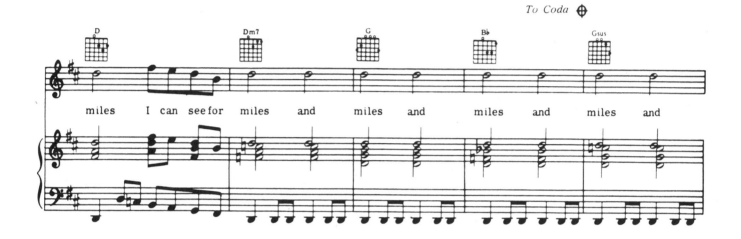

I'M FREE

Words and Music by
PETER TOWNSHEND

I CAN'T REACH YOU

Words and Music by
PETER TOWNSHEND

Moderately fast

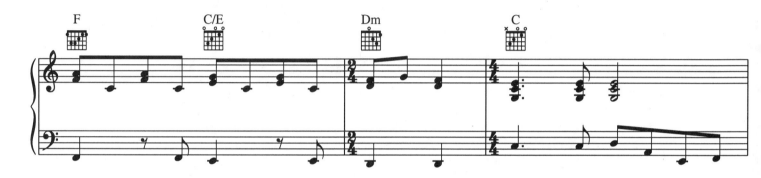

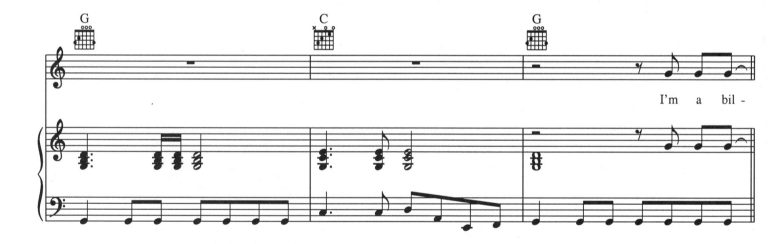

I'm a bil-

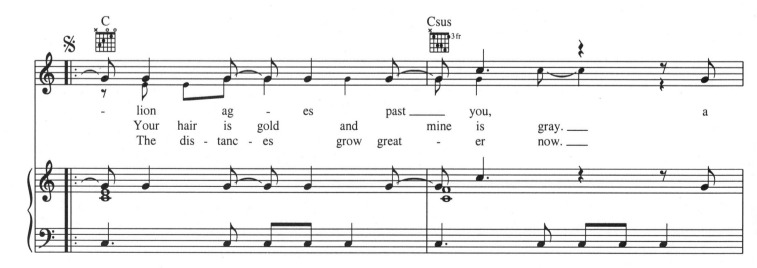

-lion ag-es past _____ you, a
Your hair is gold and mine is gray. _____
The dis-tanc-es grow great-er now. _____

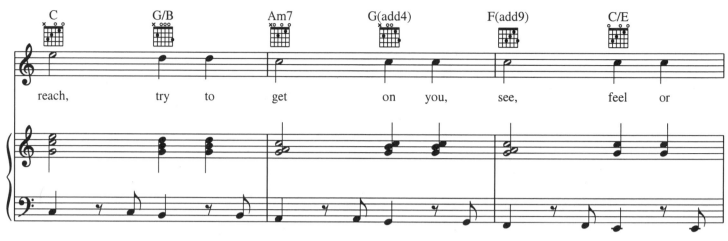

reach,   try to get   on you,   see,   feel or

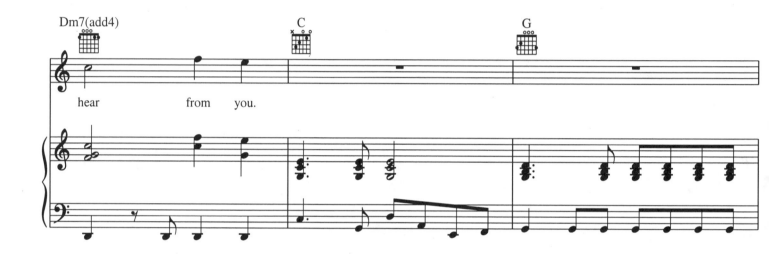

hear   from   you.

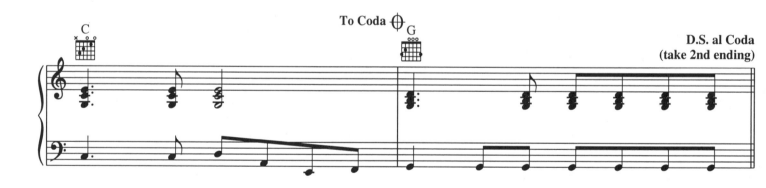

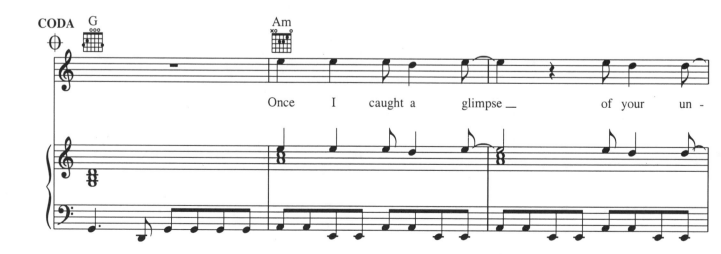

Once   I   caught a   glimpse   of your un -

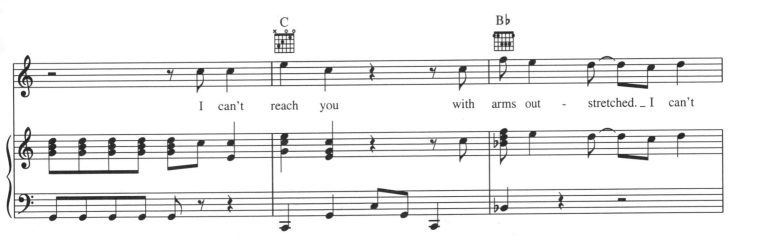

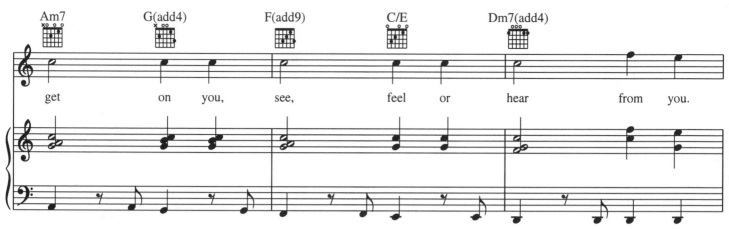

get on you, see, feel or hear from you.

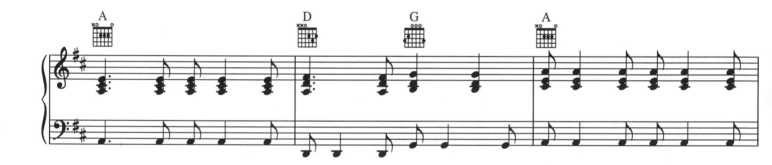

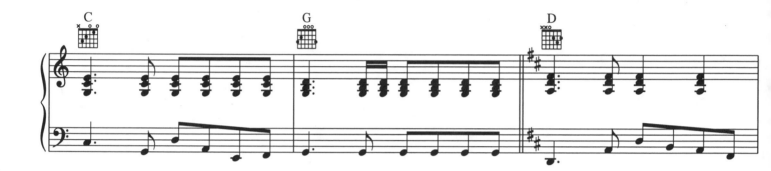

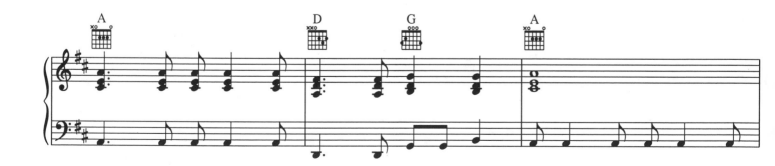

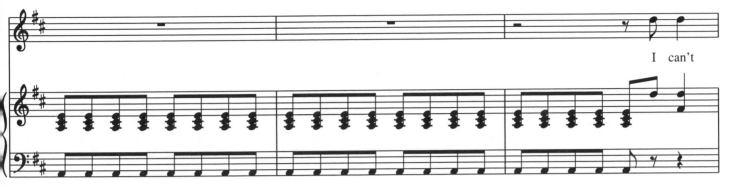

I can't

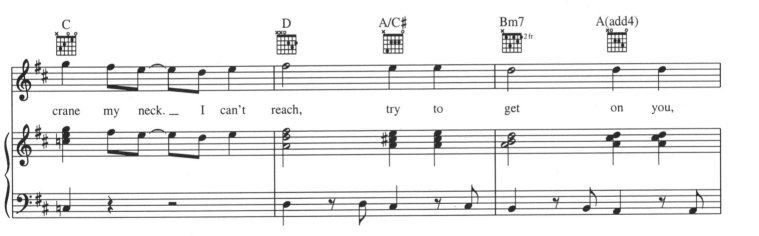

reach you   with arms out - stretched._ I can't   reach you.   I

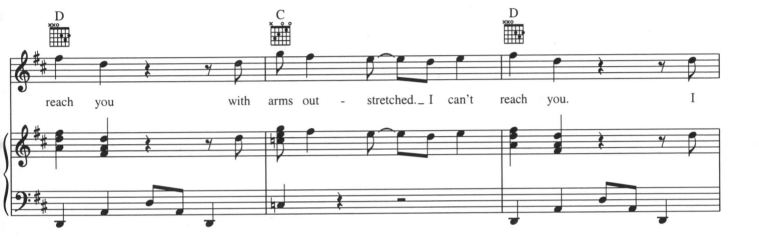

crane   my neck. _   I can't   reach,   try   to   get   on   you,

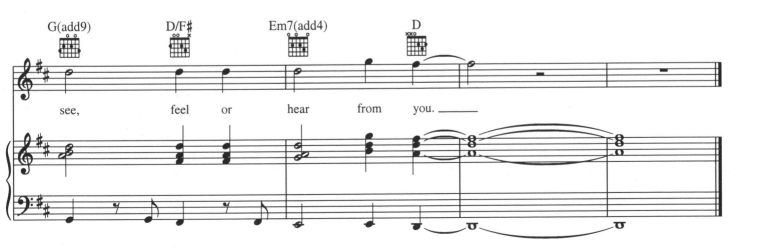

see,   feel   or   hear   from   you. _____

THE KIDS ARE ALRIGHT

Words and Music by
PETER TOWNSHEND

Moderately Bright (in 4)

I don't mind _____ oth-er guys danc-ing with my girl. _____
times, _____ I feel I got-ta get a - way. _____

That's fine, _____ I know them all pret-ty well. _____
Bells chime, _____ I know I got-ta get a - way. _____

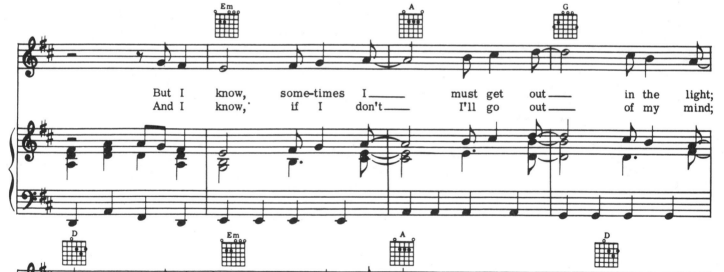

But I know, some-times I _____ must get out _____ in the light;
And I know, if I don't _____ I'll go out _____ of my mind;

_____ Bet-ter leave her be - hind _____ where The Kids Are Al - right,

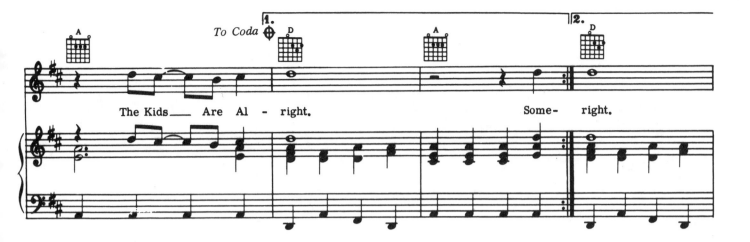

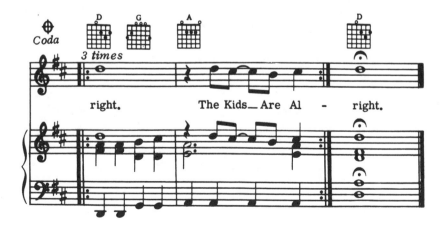

LONG LIVE ROCK

Words and Music by
PETER TOWNSHEND

Bright Rock

_____ at the As - tor - i - a the scene was _____ chang - ing.
Peo - ple walk - ing side - ways pre - tend - ing that they're leav - ing.
Place is real - ly jump - in' to the high watt amps till the

Bin - go and rock were push - ing out X - rat - ing. We were the first band to
We put on their make - up and work out all the lead - ing. Jack is in the al - ley sell - in',
twen - ty inch cym - bal fell and cut the lamps. In the black - out they danced right in -

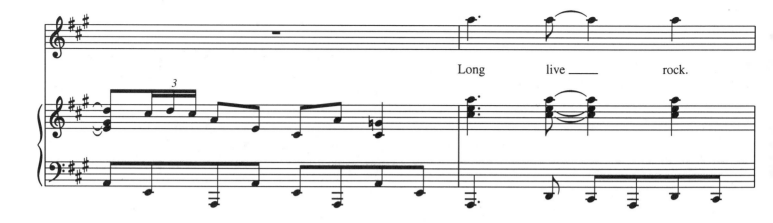

Long live ___ rock.

I need it ev-er-y night. _____

Long live ___ rock. Come on and join ___ the line. _____

Long live ___ rock _____

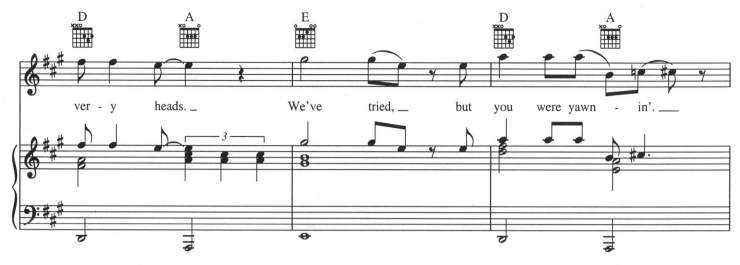

ver - y heads. ___ We've tried, ___ but you were yawn - in'. ___

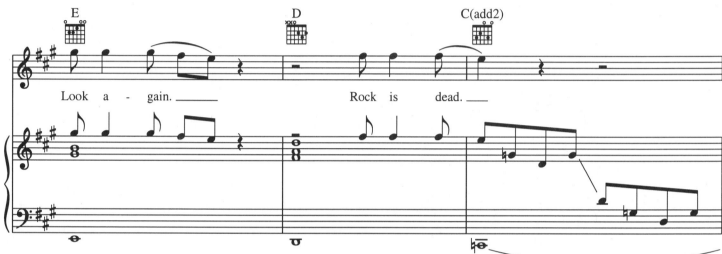

Look a - gain. _____ Rock is dead. ___

Rock is dead. _____ Rock is dead. ___

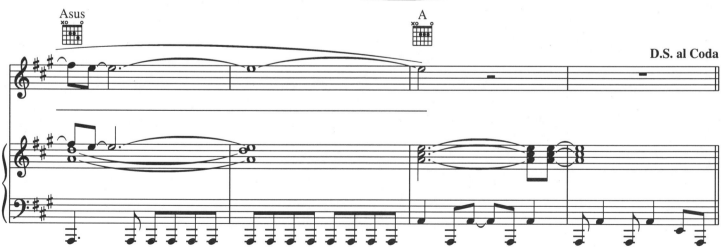

D.S. al Coda

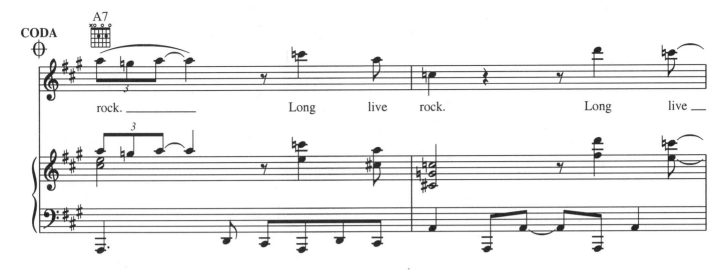

rock. _____ Long live rock. Long live _

_ rock. _ Long _ live rock. Long live _ rock.

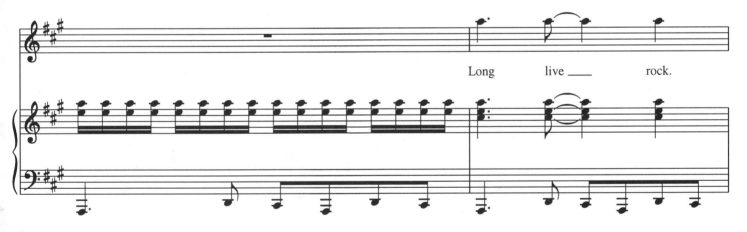

Long live ____ rock.

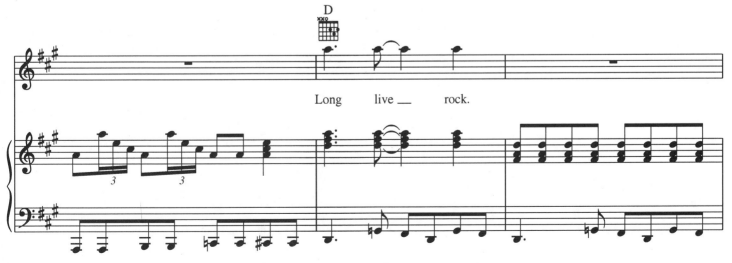

Long live _ rock.

Long live ___ rock. Long live ___ rock. ___

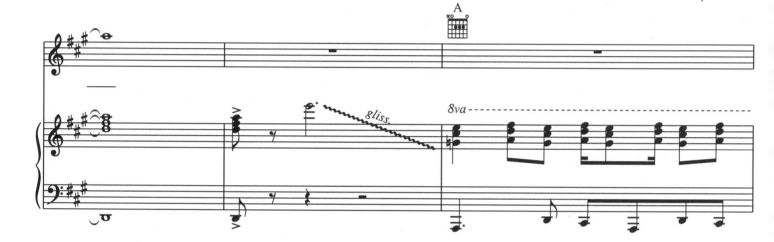

Long live ___ rock. I need it ev-er-y night. ___

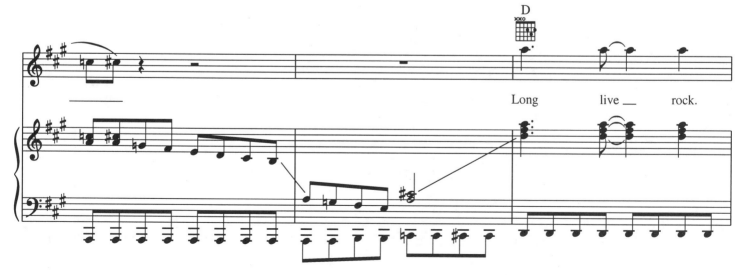

Long live ___ rock.

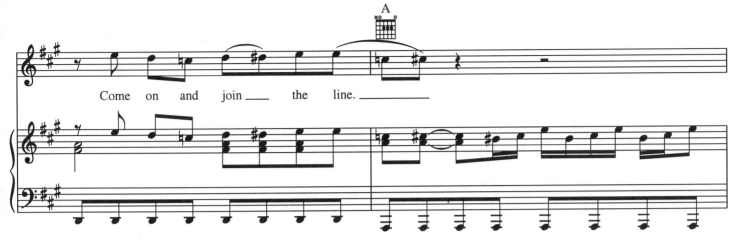

Come on and join ____ the line. _____

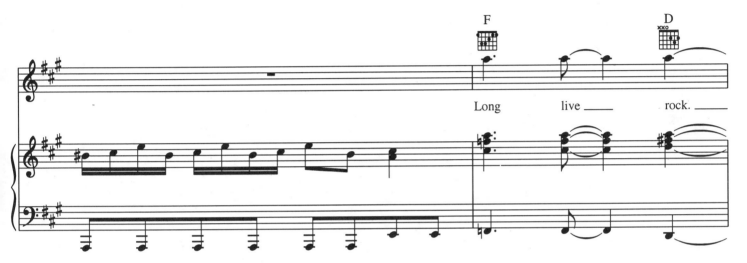

Long live ____ rock. ____

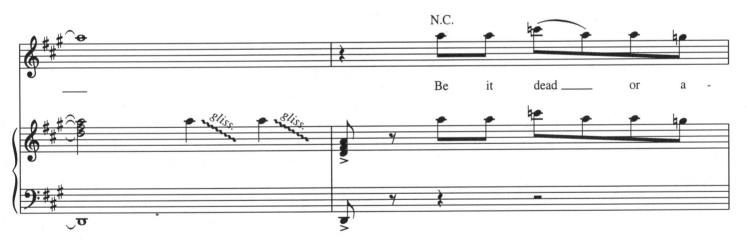

Be it dead ____ or a-

live. _____

THE MAGIC BUS

Words and Music by
PETER TOWNSHEND

house is on - ly an - oth - er mile._____ (Too much the

magic bus) Thank you driv - er for get - ting me here,_____
I don't care how much I pay,_____

Let's drive the mag - ic bus._____ You'll be an in - spec - tor,
(Too much the mag - ic bus.) Wan - na drive my bus to my

have no fear,_____ Let's drive the mag - ic bus._____
ba - by each day,_____ (Too much the mag - ic bus.)_____

I don't wish to cause a fuss,___ Let's drive the
Ev - 'ry day you would see the dust.___ (Too much the

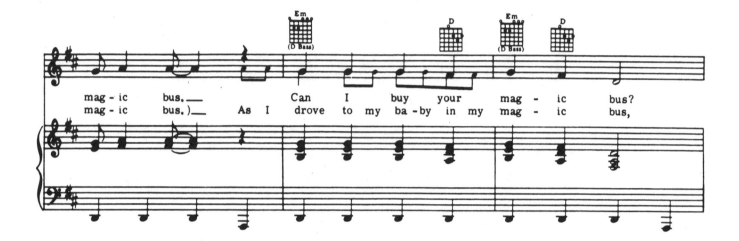

mag - ic bus.___ Can I buy your mag - ic bus?
mag - ic bus.)___ As I drove to my ba - by in my mag - ic bus,

1.
Let's drive the mag-ic bus.___
(Too much the

2.
mag - ic bus.)___

Repeat and fade

Mag-ic bus___ I want it, I want it. Mag-ic bus___ I want it, I want it.

MY GENERATION

Words and Music by
PETER TOWNSHEND

Moderately

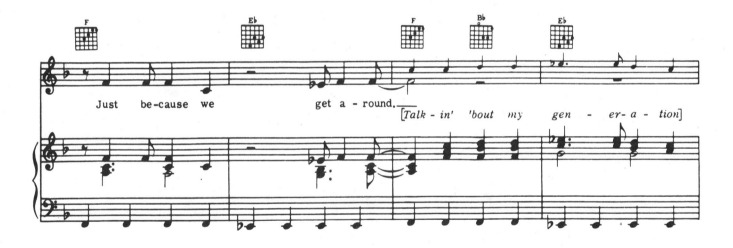

People try to put us down___ [Talk - in' 'bout my gen - er - a - tion]

Just be-cause we get a - round.___ [Talk - in' 'bout my gen - er - a - tion]

Things they do look aw - ful cold.___ [Talk - in' 'bout my gen - er - a - tion]

Hope I die be-fore__ I get old. [Talk - in' 'bout my gen - er - a - tion] This is my gen-er-

a - tion,__ This is my gen-er - a - tion, ba - by.__

Why don't__ you all fade__ a - way?__ [Talk - in' 'bout my gen - er - a - tion]

Don't try and dig what we all say.__ [Talk - in' 'bout my gen - er - a - tion] I'm

not tryin' to cause a big sen - sa - tion. I'm just
[Talk - in' 'bout my gen - er - a - tion]

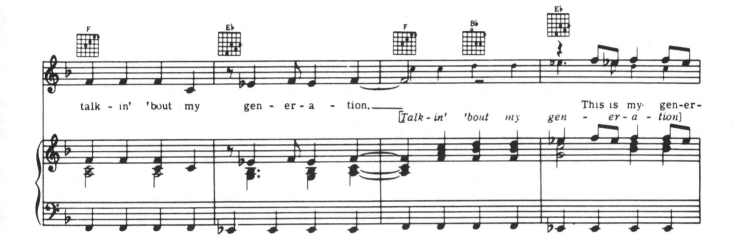

talk - in' 'bout my gen - er - a - tion.___ This is my gen - er -
[Talk - in' 'bout my gen - er - a - tion]

a - tion,___ This is my gen - er - a - tion, ba - by._____

MY WIFE

Words and Music by
JOHN ENTWISTLE

Bright Rock

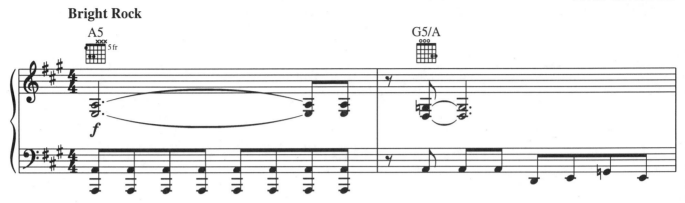

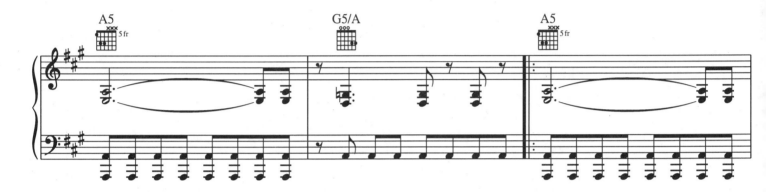

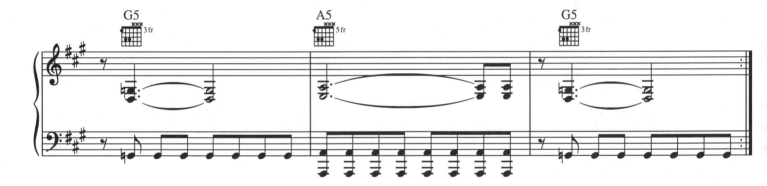

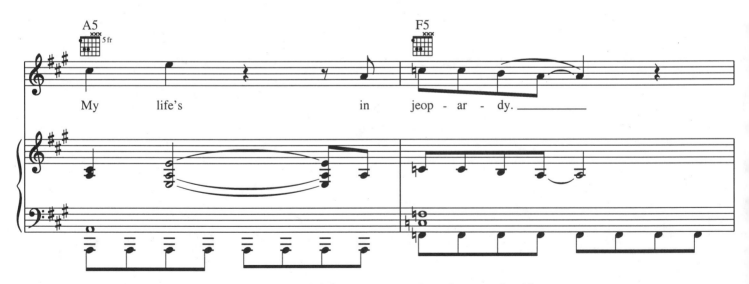

My life's in jeop - ar - dy. _____

Original key: B major. This edition has been transposed down one step in order to be more playable.

num-ber one. ___ Give me a bo-dy-guard,_ a black belt

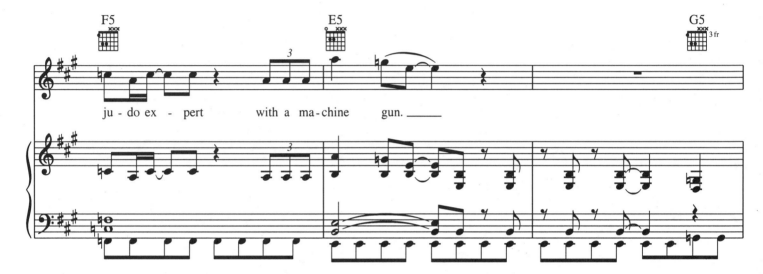

ju - do ex - pert with a ma-chine gun. _____

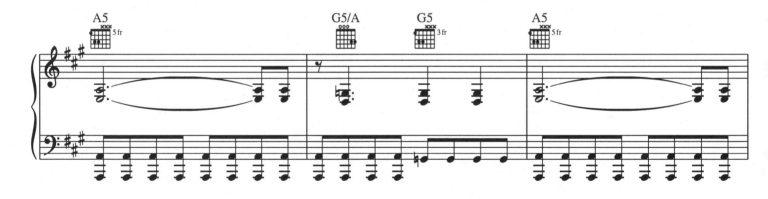

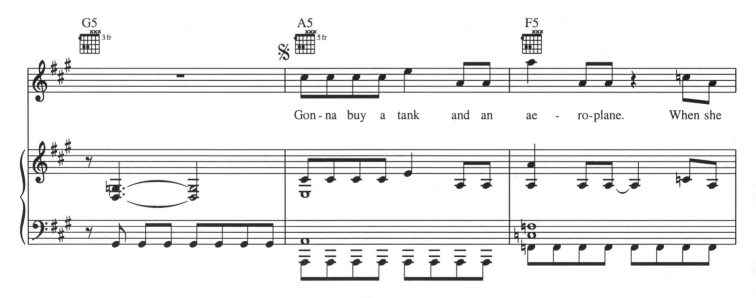

Gon-na buy a tank and an ae-ro-plane. When she

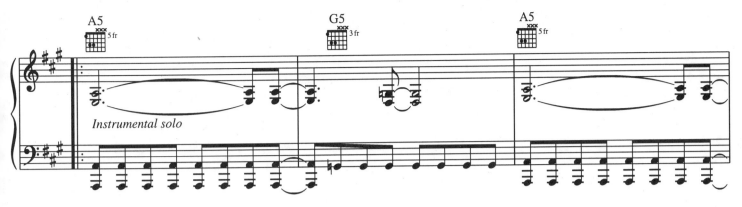

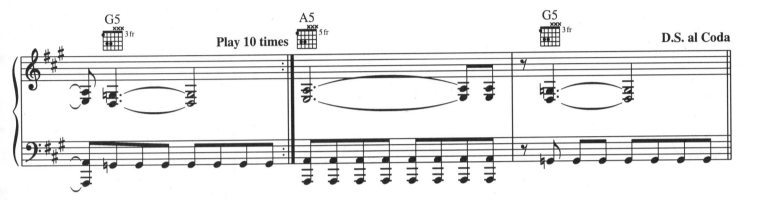

And I'm oh so tired of run - ning, gon - na lay down on ___ the floor. ___ I got - ta rest some time, so

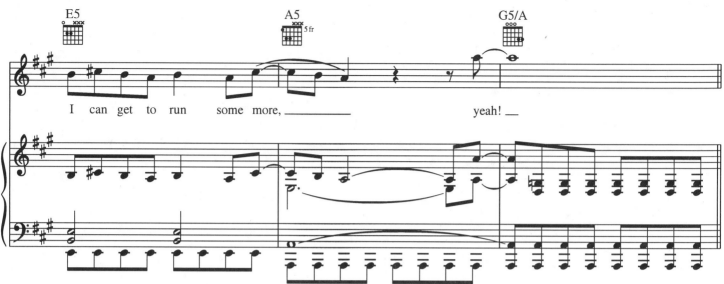

I can get to run some more, _____ yeah! _____

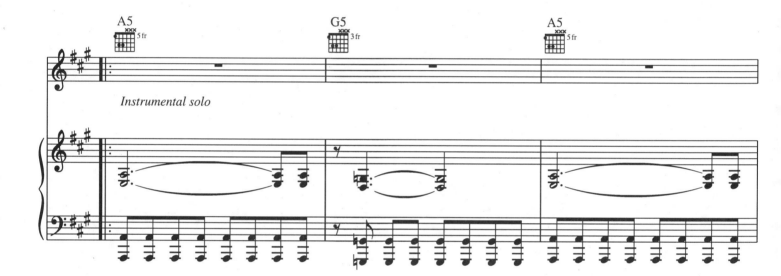

Instrumental solo

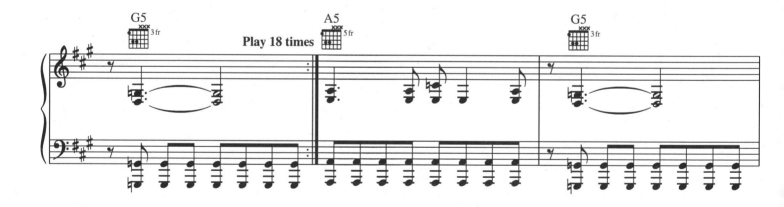

Play 18 times

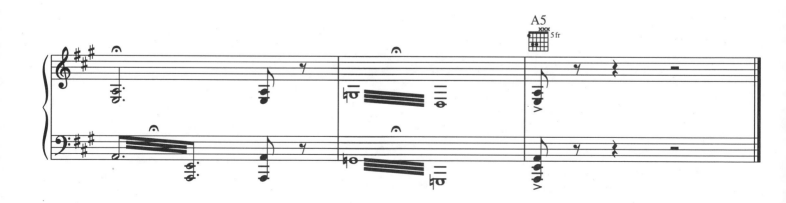

PINBALL WIZARD

Words and Music by
PETER TOWNSHEND

1. Ev-er since I was a young boy_____ I
stands_____ like a stat-ue,_____ be-comes
Ain't got no dis-trac-tions,_____ can't
4. He's been on my fav-'rite tab-le,

THE REAL ME

Words and Music by
PETER TOWNSHEND

Medium Rock beat

I went back __ to the doc - tor __ to get an - oth - er shrink. __

__ I say there, __ tell him 'bout __ my week - end __ but he nev -

er be-trays__ what he thinks.____ Can you see__ the real__

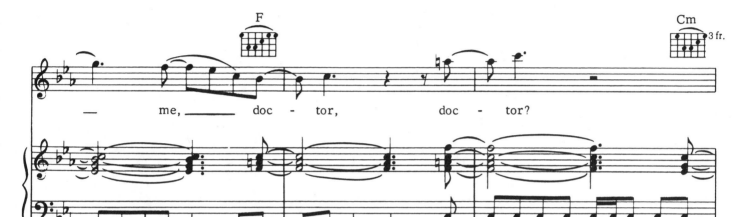

__ me,____ doc - tor, doc - tor?

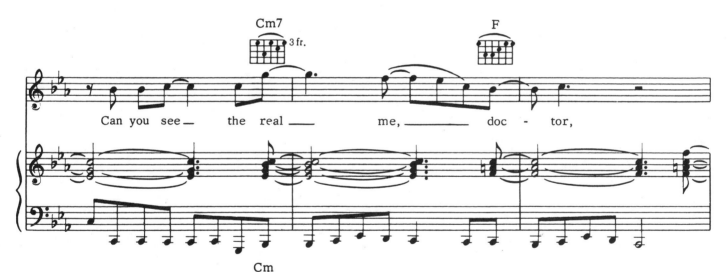

Can you see__ the real____ me,____ doc - tor,

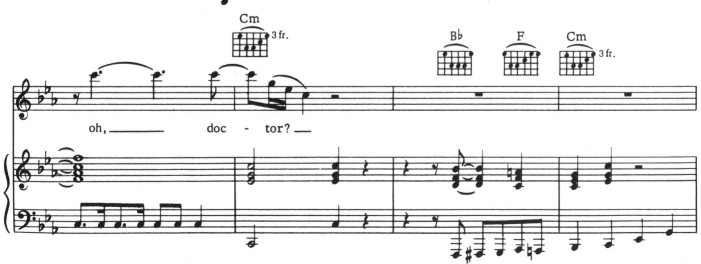

oh,_____ doc - tor? __

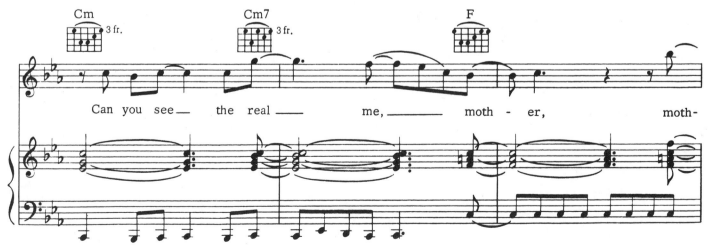

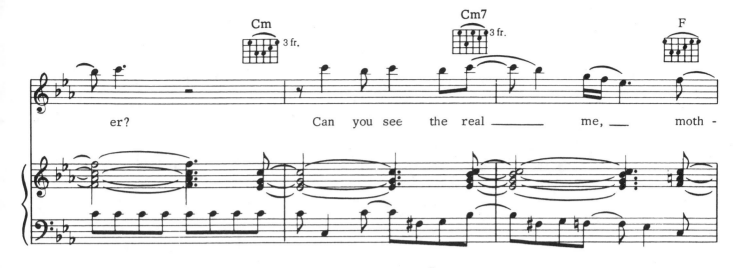

er?   Can you see the real _____ me, ___ moth -

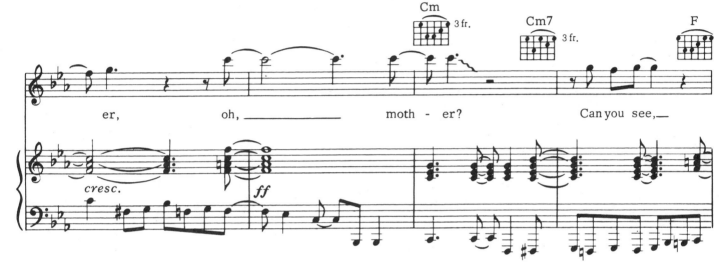

er,   oh, _____ moth - er?   Can you see,___

can you see, ___   can you see the real me? ___   Can you see,___

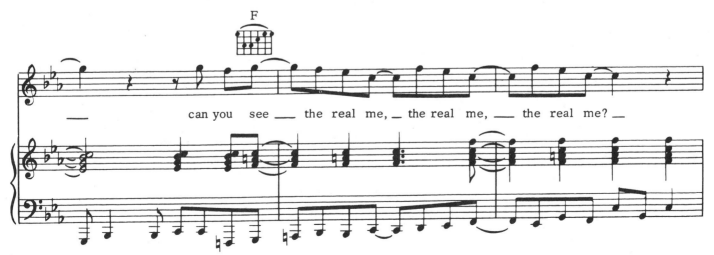

___   can you see ___ the real me, ___ the real me, ___ the real me? ___

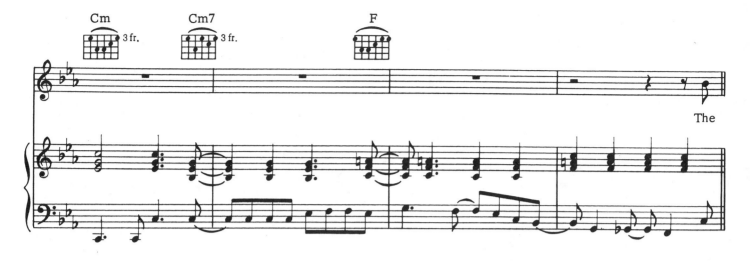

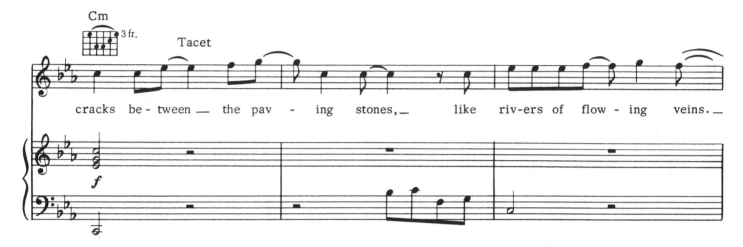

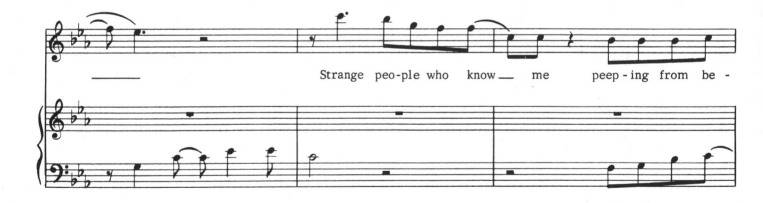

me, _____ preach - er, preach - er?

Can you see the real _____ me, _____ preach - er?

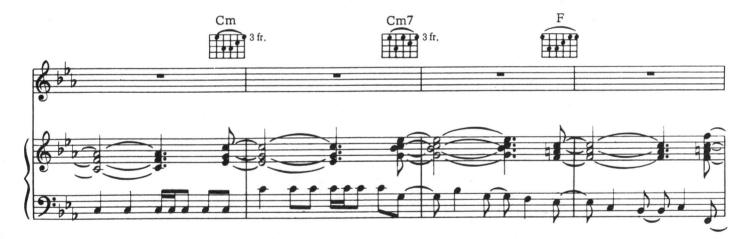

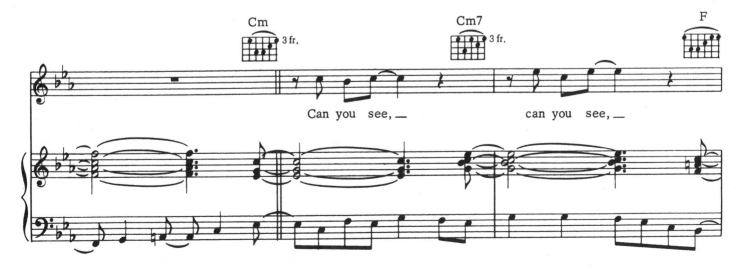

Can you see, _____ can you see, _____

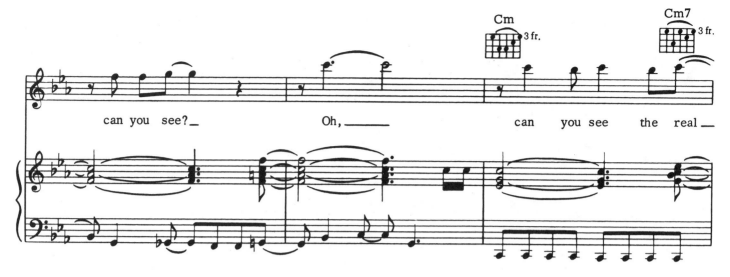

can you see?__ Oh,____ can you see the real__

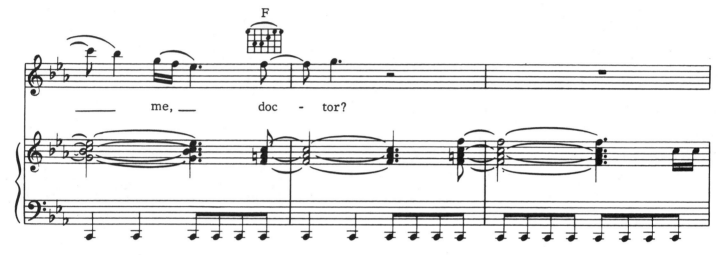

__ me,__ doc - tor?

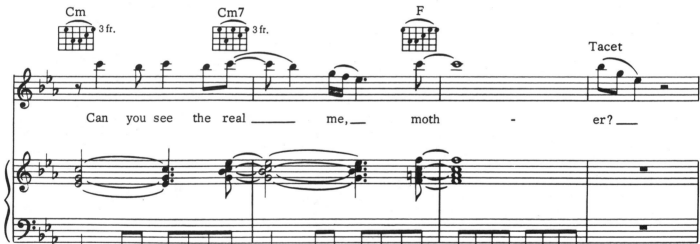

Can you see the real ____ me,__ moth - er?__

Can you see __ the real me,___ me, me, me, me, me, me, me, me?

THE SEEKER

Words and Music by
PETER TOWNSHEND

Moderate Rock

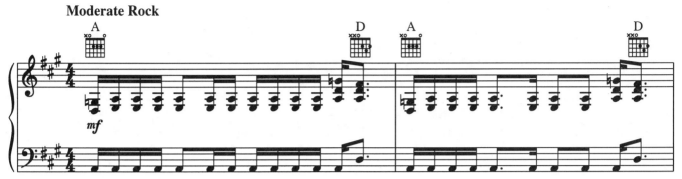

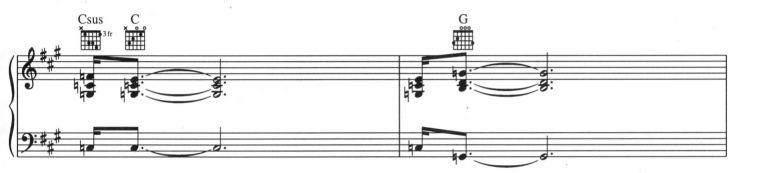

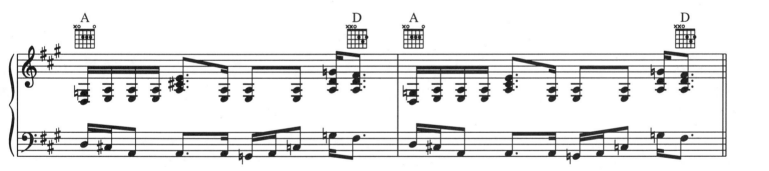

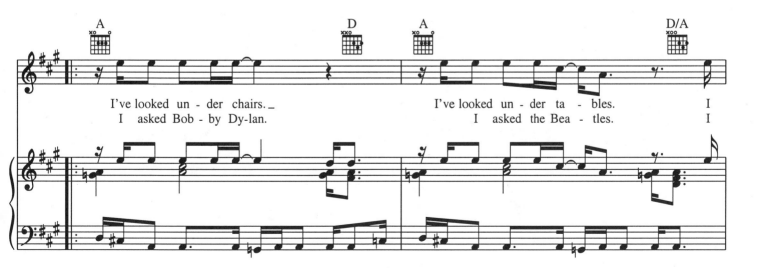

I've looked un-der chairs. _ I've looked un-der ta - bles. I
I asked Bob-by Dy-lan. I asked the Bea - tles. I

tried to find __ the key __ to fif - ty mil - lion fa - bles.
asked Tim-o-thy Lear-y __ but he could-n't help me ei - ther. } They call me the

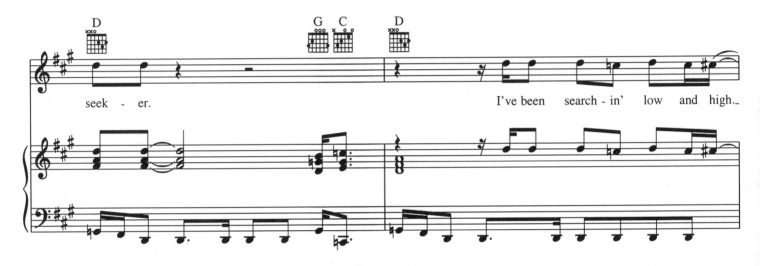

seek - er. I've been search - in' low and high. __

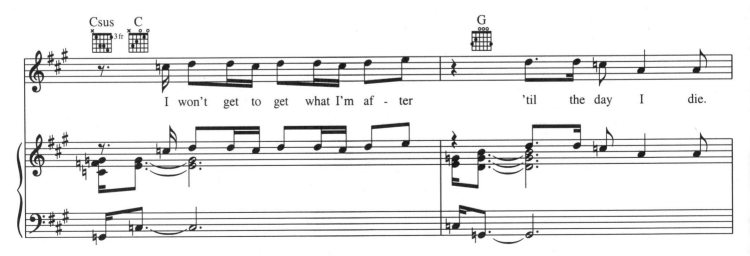

I won't get to get what I'm af - ter 'til the day I die.

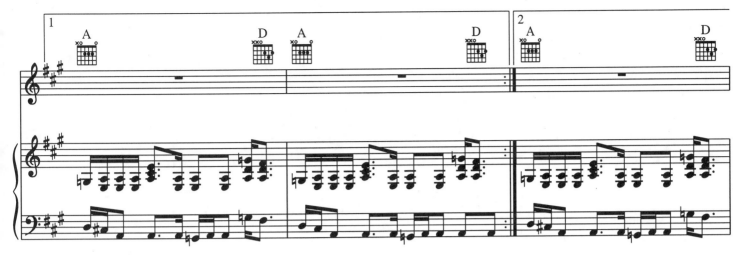

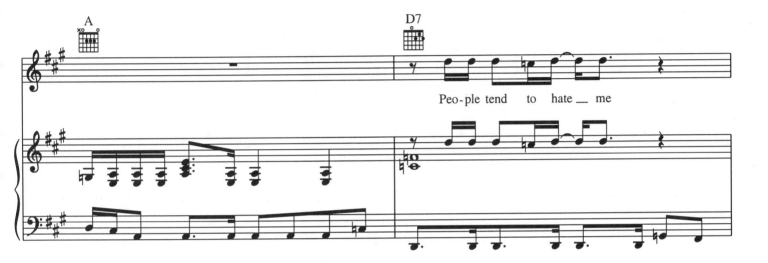

Peo-ple tend to hate __ me

'cause I nev - er smile.____ As I ran - sack __ their homes __ they wan-na shake my hand.__

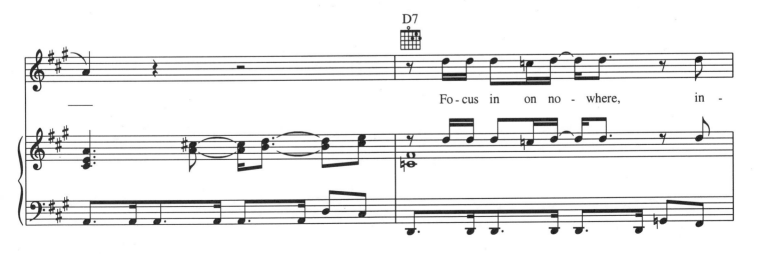

____ Fo - cus in on no - where, in -

ves - ti - gat - in' miles. _ I'm a seek - er. I'm a real - ly des - per - ate man.

I won't get to get what I'm af-ter 'til the day I die.

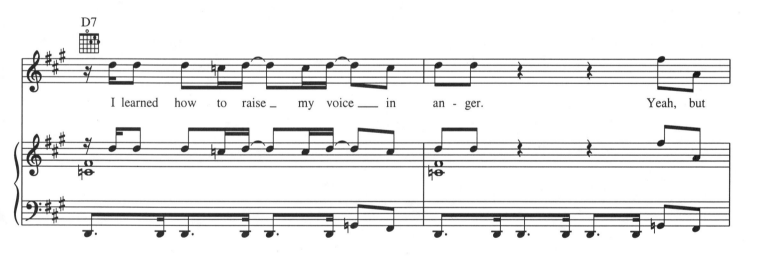

I learned how to raise my voice in an-ger. Yeah, but

look at my face, ain't this a smile? I'm

hap - py when life's good and when it's bad __ I cry. __ I've got

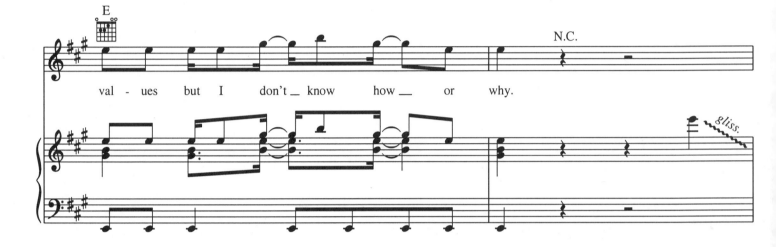

val - ues but I don't __ know how __ or why.

I'm look - in' for me. __ You're look - in' for you. __ We're

look - in' in at each oth - er and we don't know what to do. __ They call me the

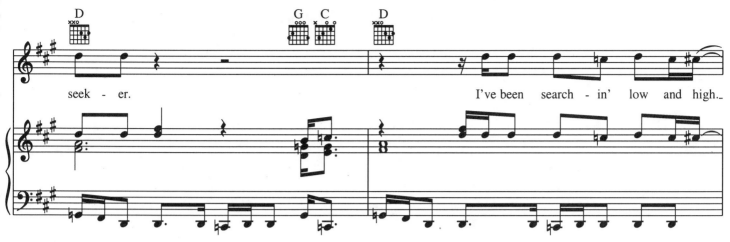

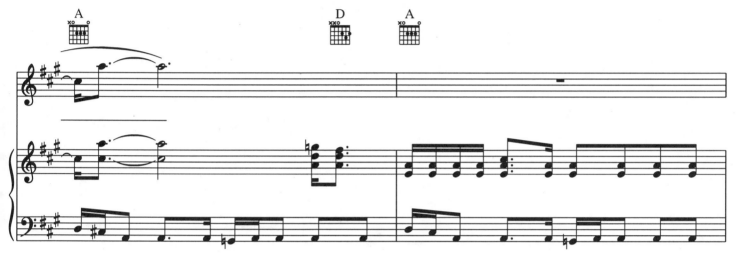

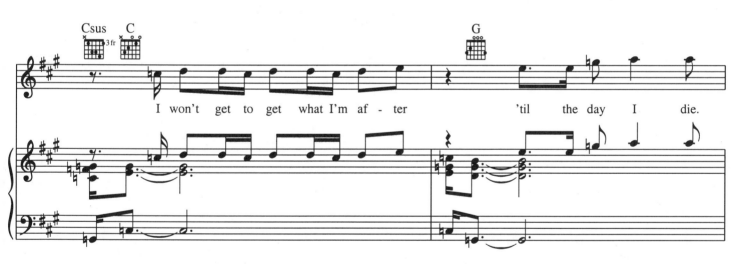

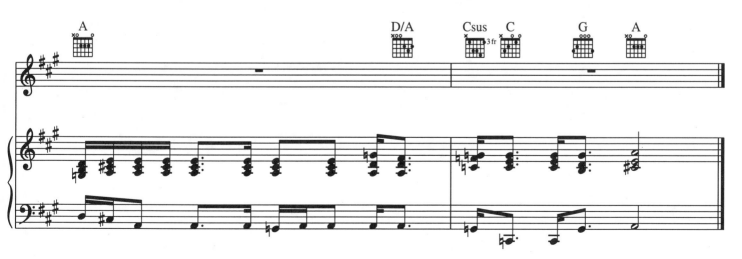

SQUEEZE BOX

Words and Music by
PETER TOWNSHEND

Medium Rock beat

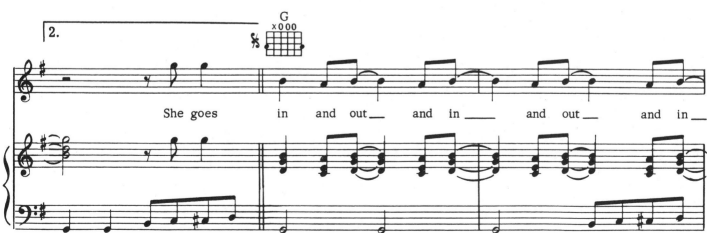

squeeze me. _____ Come on ____ and tease me like you

do, I'm so in love with you. _____ Ma -

ma's got a squeeze box, Dad - dy nev-er sleeps at night. ____

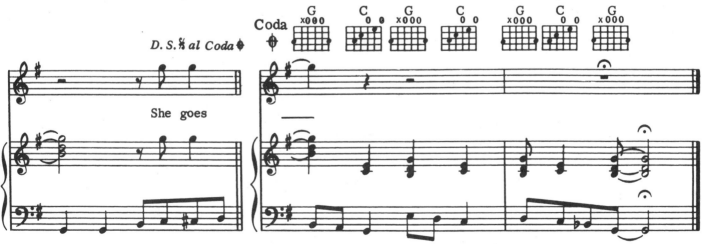

D. S. al Coda

Coda

She goes

SUBSTITUTE

Words and Music by
PETER TOWNSHEND

Bright Rock

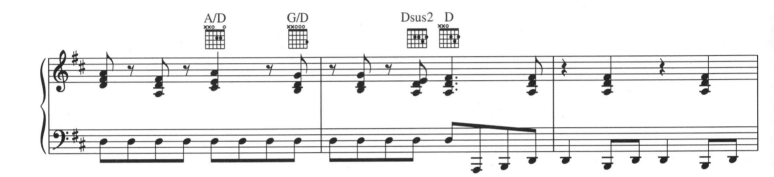

(1.) You think we look pret-ty good to-geth-er._____

(2.,3.) I was born with a plas-tic spoon in my ___ mouth. _

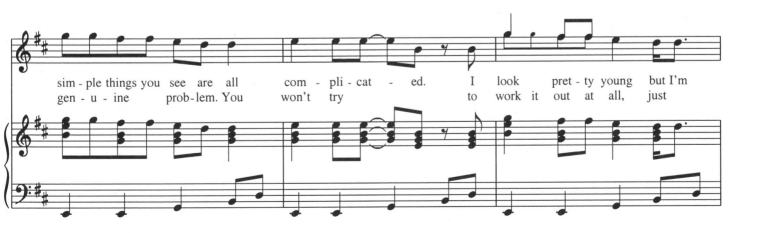

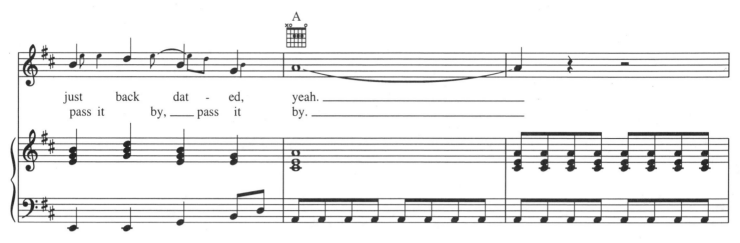

just back dat - ed, yeah. _____
pass it by, ___ pass it by. _____

Sub - sti - tute your lies for fact. I see right through your
Sub - sti - tute me for him. Sub - sti - tute my

plas - tic, Mac. I look all white but my dad was black. My
coke for gin. Sub - sti - tute you for my mum. At

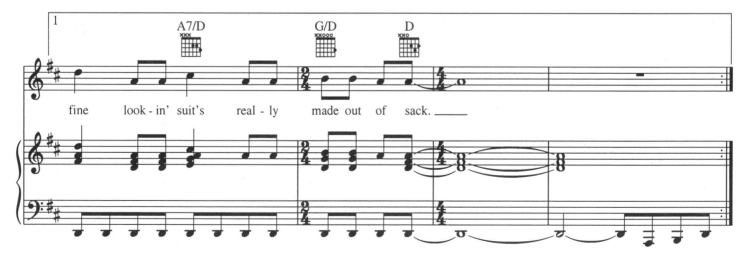

fine look - in' suit's real - ly made out of sack. ____

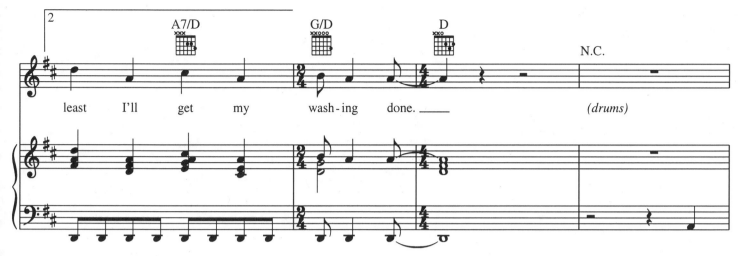

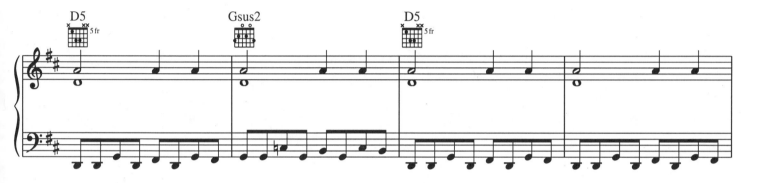

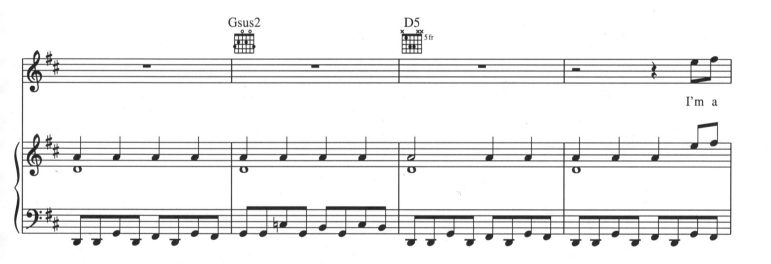

heels are high. The sim-ple things you see are all com-pli-cat - ed. I

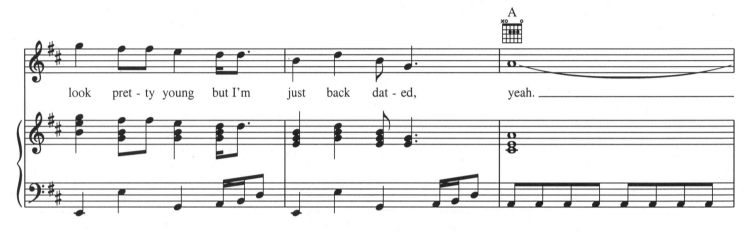

look pret-ty young but I'm just back dat-ed, yeah. _____

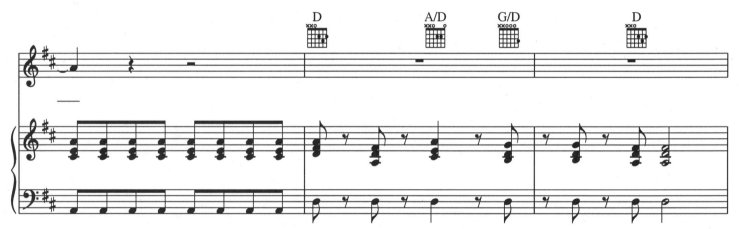

D.S. al Coda

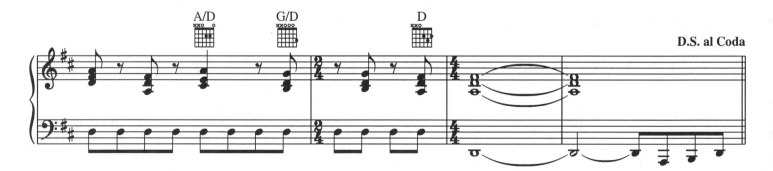

CODA

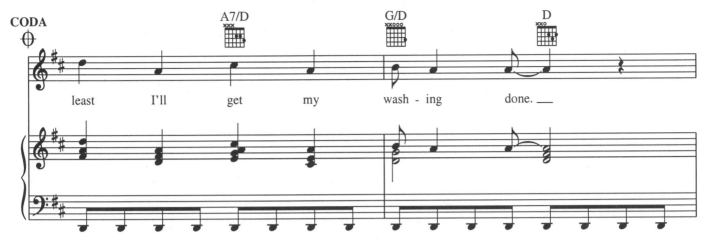

least I'll get my wash-ing done. __

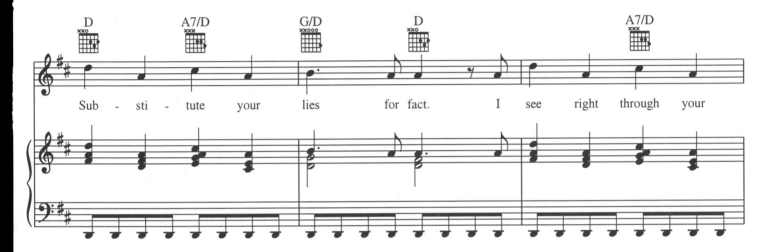

Sub-sti-tute your lies for fact. I see right through your

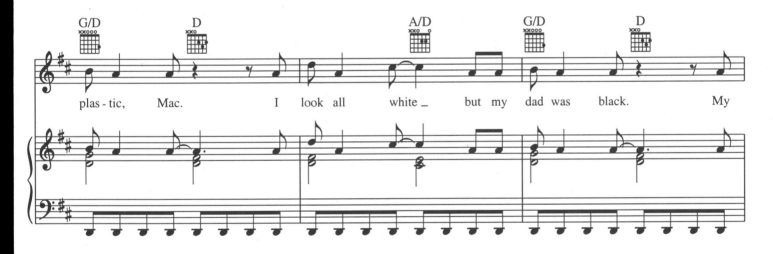

plas-tic, Mac. I look all white __ but my dad was black. My

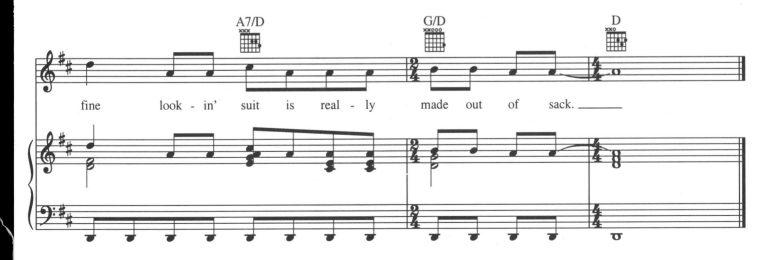

fine look-in' suit is real-ly made out of sack. _____

WHO ARE YOU

Words and Music by
PETER TOWNSHEND

Bright Rock Beat

Who____ are____ you? Who, who, who, who?

Who_____ are____ you? Who, who, who, who?

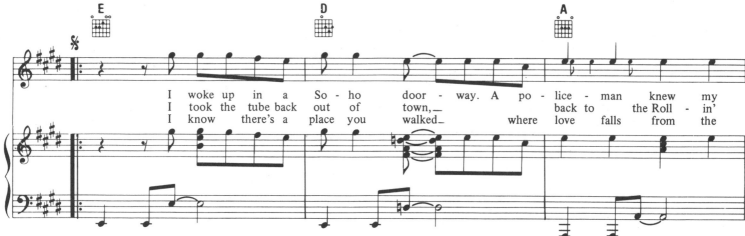

I woke up in a So - ho door - way. A po - lice - man knew my
I took the tube back out of town,____ back to the Roll - in'
I know there's a place you walked____ where love falls from the

name. He said, "You can go____ sleep at home____ to - night____ if you can
Pin. I felt a lit - tle like a dy - ing clown____ with a
trees. My heart____ is like a bro - ken cup.____ I on - ly

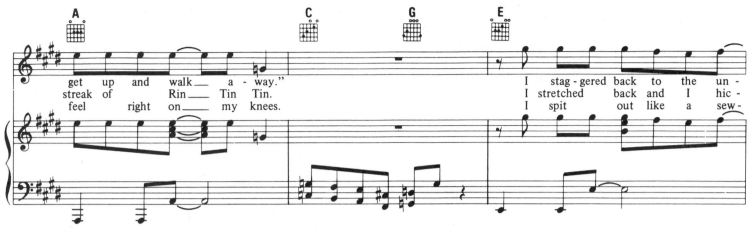

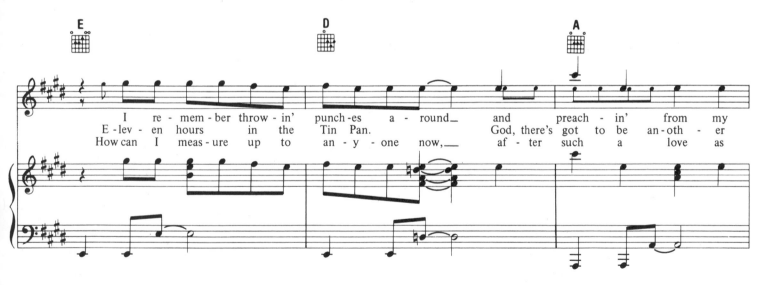

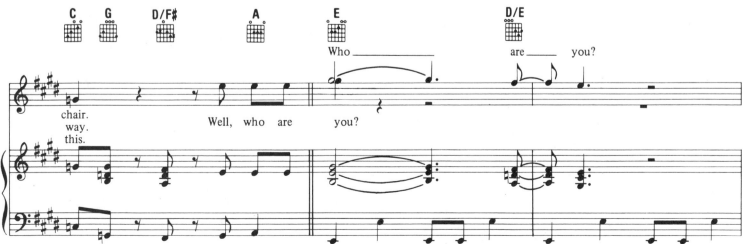

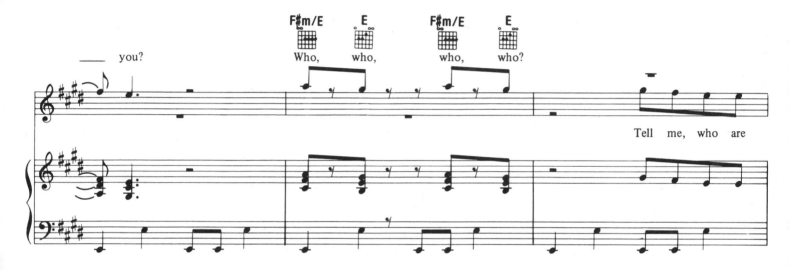

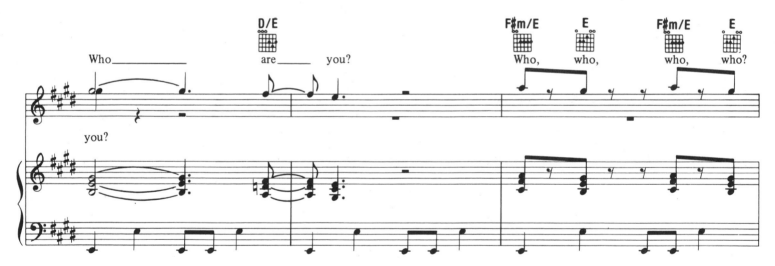

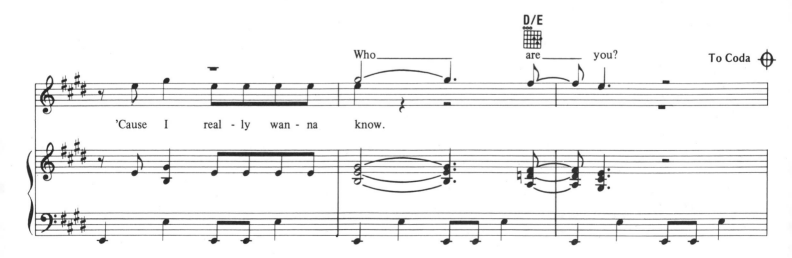

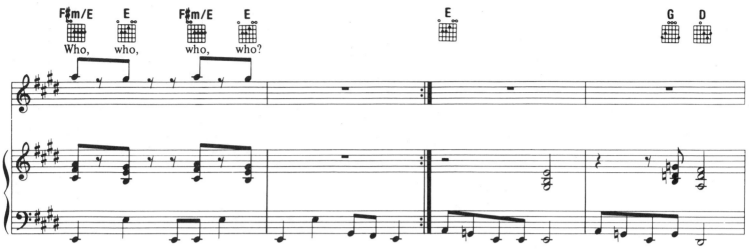

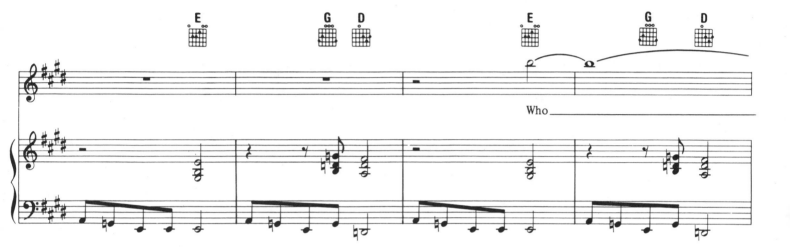

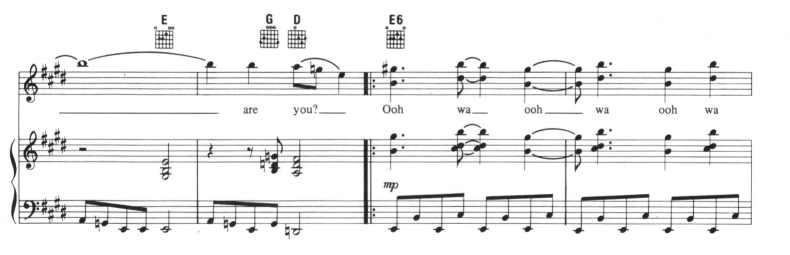

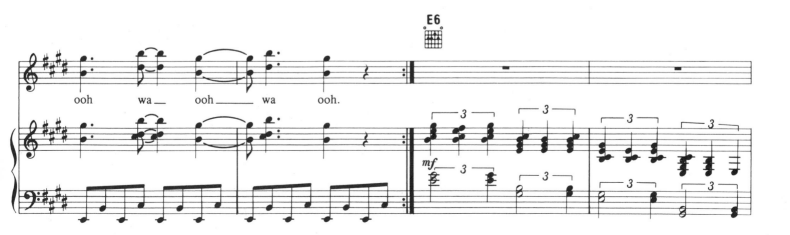

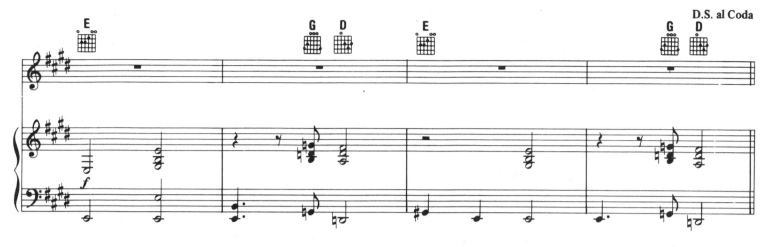

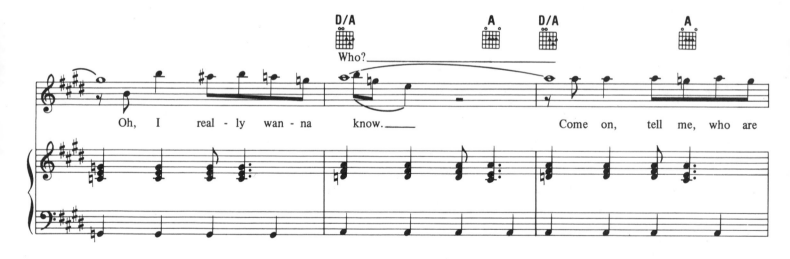

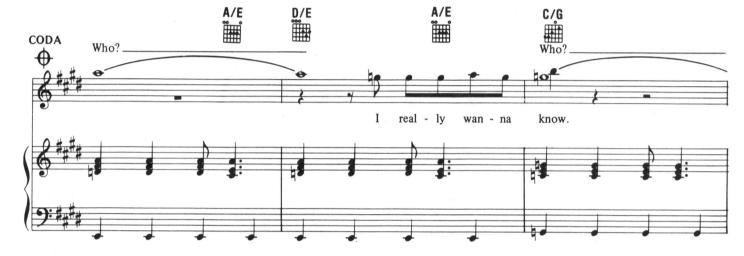

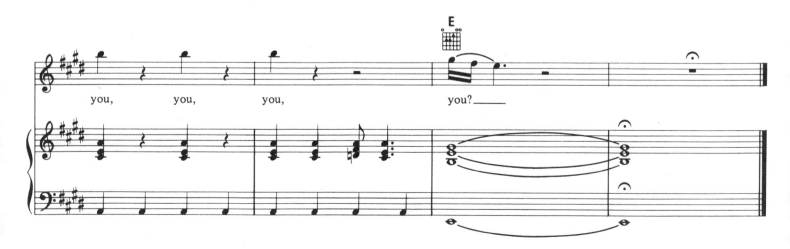

WON'T GET FOOLED AGAIN

Words and Music by
PETER TOWNSHEND

gun sings the song.__
in the last war.__
er ov - er -night.__

I'll tip my hat__ to the new con-sti-tu-tion;

Take a bow__ for the new re-vo-lu-tion; Smile and grin__ at the change all a-round; Pick up my gui-tar and play,

__ Just like yes-ter-day.__ Then I'll get on my knees and pray.

To Coda

We don't get fooled__ a - gain.__

I'll move my-self and my fam-'ly a-side___ If we hap-pen to be left half a-live;

Get all my pa-pers and smile___at the sky, Tho' I know that the hyp-no-tized nev-er lie.

1.

2. The

2.

D. S. al Coda

3. There's

Coda

Meet the new___Boss! same as the old Boss!

NC

YOU BETTER YOU BET

Words and Music by
PETER TOWNSHEND

Medium Rock

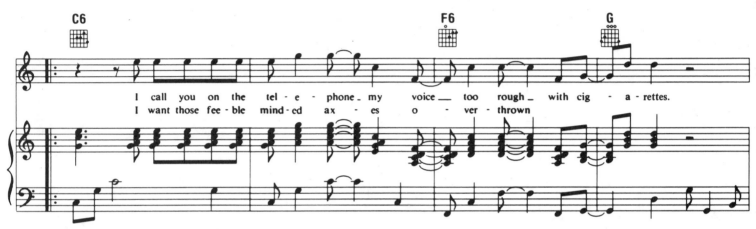

I call you on the tel-e-phone my voice__ too rough__ with cig-a-rettes.
I want those fee-ble mind-ed ax-es o-ver-thrown

I some-times feel I should just__ go home. but I'm deal-ing with a mem-o-ry that nev-er for-gets.__
I'm not in-to your__ pass-port pic-ture I just__ like__ your__ nose.

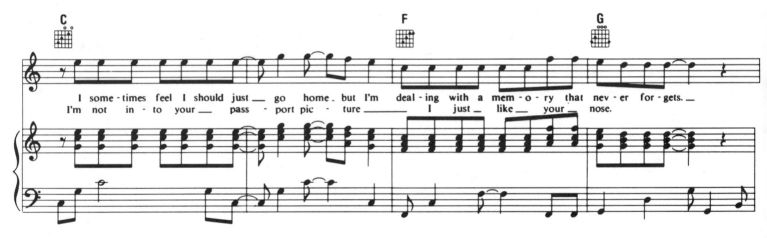

I love to hear you say__ my name__ es-pec-ial-ly when you__ say yes.__
You wel-come me with o-pen arms__ and o-pen legs,

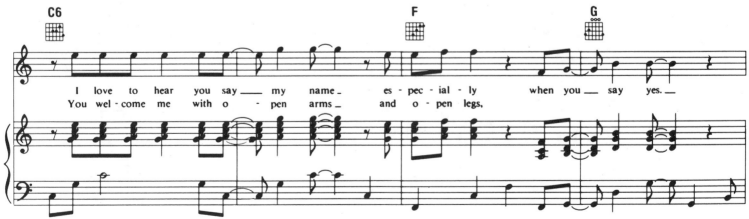

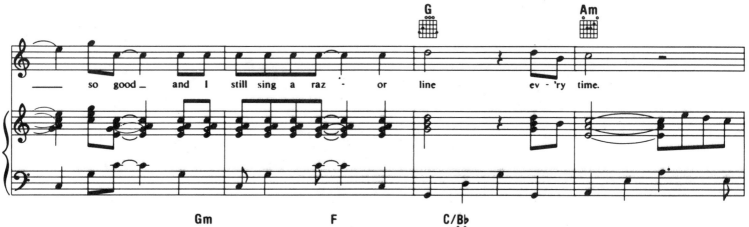

so good __ and I still sing a raz - or line ev - 'ry time.

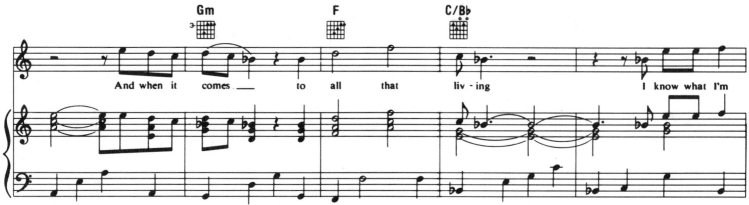

And when it comes __ to all that liv - ing I know what I'm

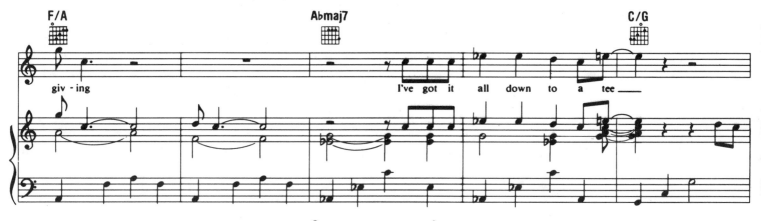

giv - ing I've got it all down to a tee __

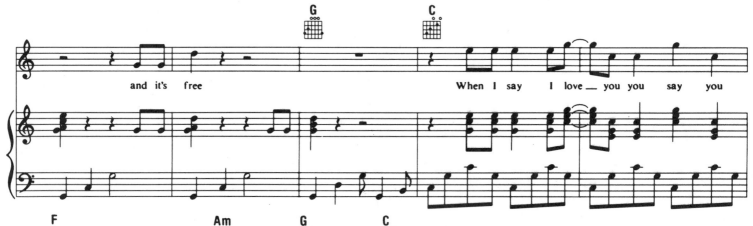

and it's free When I say I love __ you you say you

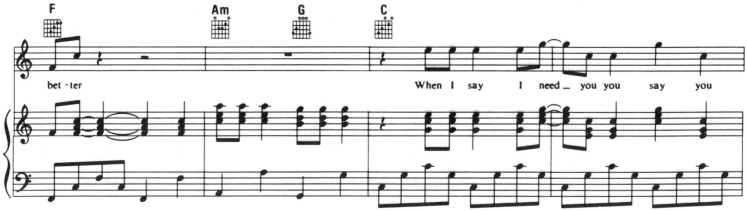

bet - ter When I say I need __ you you say you